*f***P**

Motherland

A Memoir

PAMELA MARIN

Free Press
New York • London • Toronto • Sydney

*f*P

FREE PRESS
A Division of Simon & Schuster, Inc.
1230 Avenue of the Americas
New York, NY 10020

For information regarding special discounts for bulk purchases, please contact Simon & Schuster Special Sales at 1-800-456-6798 or business@simonandschuster.com.

Manufactured in the United States of America

10   9   8   7   6   5   4   3   2   1

Library of Congress Cataloging-in-Publication Data
Marin, Pamela.
    Motherland / a memoir.
        p. cm.
        1. Marin, Pamela, 1958–. 2. Marin, Mildred, 1923–1973. 3. Journalists—United States—Biography. 4. Mothers and daughters—United States—Biography.
CT275.M198 A3 2005
206.874'3'092273—dc22   *2004061931*

ISBN 0-7432-5610-7

Motherland

Sometimes I pretend my mother is watching me. I use her, the thought of her, if I think I might say something or do something in a situation that doesn't require me to say or do, like a parent-teacher conference at preschool. Before I go into the classroom, to sit on a midget chair at a knee-high table and listen to a childless twenty-seven-year-old tell me about one of my kids, I might bring a picture of my mom to mind, and for a meditative moment feel that by placing her between myself and the world I will acquire the dignity and grace I ascribe to her.

But I can't hold the thought. I can never hold the thought. I see my mother sitting peacefully, with her faraway stillness, her useful hands folded in her lap, then the image fades and I say something that signals my impatience.

My mother is an idea to me, like God. And like a god she has been an ideal repository for my anger and accusations, my love and longing, for my shape-shifting images of myself. Her name was Mildred Elizabeth Lady until she was twenty-eight years old, when she married my father and became Mrs. Allan Marin. More than half her life was over by the time she shed her given names, the better half, it seems to me now, as I near the age she was when she died.

I was fourteen when my mother died of breast cancer. She was fifty. She had been sick for years but never told me so, and I didn't see her during the last months of her life, which she spent alone in California, two thousand miles from our home in Evanston, Illinois, two thousand miles from her husband, her children, and her own mother, who lived with us.

She died in 1973, before breast cancer walkathons and pink breast cancer lapel ribbons and breast-cancer-surviving celebrities splashed into the news. It was the year Nixon's criminals testified in Congress, and the last U.S. troops left Vietnam. I have come to understand the times as I will never be able to understand my mother. Most of what I know about her I learned when I researched her life as I would a stranger's. I was twenty-nine. I'd been working at a newspaper in California—following leads, conducting interviews, tapping out a thousand-word story per week, give or take. I liked being a reporter better than working as a waitress or a secretary, the jobs that were my undergrad and doctoral prep for journalism. "What's your angle?" I was often asked by those I interviewed, usually the ones with angles of their own. The question grated. I saw myself as a fact finder, an observer. Yes, everyone has a point of view, but reporters generally aim for fairness, and libel law generally enforces it.

I slipped through the looking glass when I dug into my mother's story.

Professional decorum? I wept in every interview. Sometimes my emotions carried me so far from the job at hand that my interview subjects wrapped their arms around me and soothed me as if I were a colicky baby. Objectivity? I leapt at scraps of hearsay. This one says my grandfather hid a bottle in his desk at the factory? In an instant I reconfigured my mother's biography, attributing her fall into my teetotaling father's arms to her dad's drunkenness. Fifty people told me of her kindness before one described her as cold and selfish and confessed a wicked prank her schoolmates played on her. Get me rewrite: First I was eerily thrilled by the tidbit, as if it let me off the hook for not knowing much about my mom. Her life was a blank canvas to me *because she was cold.* Her fault. Then I felt sad for her—the outcast schoolgirl cruelly tricked—and sadder for my own schoolgirl self, who hadn't the warmth to warm her own mother. Finally I was angry at the old woman who poured that poison in my ear.

By the time I was making my first memories, my mother was in the last decade of her life. It was the sixties, and we were a suburban family of five: mother and father, sister and brother, and widowed grandmother quietly crocheting in a rocker upstairs. We opened presents under a fir tree on Christmas mornings. We shared our big brown Thanksgiving turkeys and clove-speckled Easter hams with our cousins from Chicago's southside. Sunday mornings, we piled into our Cadillac and my father drove us half a mile to the only block in Evanston that housed two stone churches—the First Baptist Church, and the First Church of Christ, Scientist. Hers and his. I went with my mother and grandmother to the Baptists, while my father took my brother to hear the gospel according to Mary Baker Eddy.

When my mom died, our family traditions disappeared with her.

My father shipped my grandmother—his mother-in-law—back to Tennessee. He got rid of my mother's clothes and emptied her shelves in the bathroom. He worked long hours at his office in the Loop and traveled for business, leaving his teenage children alone with their teen troubles. He started dating.

Five years after he was widowed, my father went bankrupt and moved in with his girlfriend. He was sixty-six. She was thirty-six. I was nineteen. He put my mother's wedding ring on her finger, though they never married, and gave her my mother's jewelry. The bits of furniture and art he'd saved from creditors went with him to his girlfriend's high-rise apartment near the stretch of Michigan Avenue that civic boosters call the Magnificent Mile.

Christmases and Thanksgivings and Easters I was invited to her apartment to sit at the table from our house in Evanston and eat food she prepared in my mother's hammered copper pots, served on my mother's china, using my mother's silver—laid on a lace tablecloth crocheted by my grandmother, who had moved North to live with us when I was born, and died in a nursing home in Tennessee.

After I began poking around my mother's life, I wasn't invited over anymore.

"Why are you doing this to me?" my father yelled at me one sunny day in 1988, when I was a twenty-nine-year-old reporter following leads, conducting interviews—researching my mother's life.

"To *you?*" I said, wondering what he'd buried that he didn't want exhumed. That was one of the last times we spoke.

He stayed with his thirty-years-younger girlfriend until he died at the age of eighty-six, in 1999, more than a decade after I went looking for my mom. When we lived in Evanston he was a church usher, dressed in gray-striped usher's pants every Sunday, a fresh carnation on his lapel, and that was one tradition he held on to after family life went belly-up. My father the lifelong Christian Scientist continued his weekly religious duties at a church near his girlfriend's apartment. Yet he battled his own cancer with the help of doctors at one of Chicago's best hospitals. And he died at home, in his girlfriend's bed, with her at his side tending him with morphine from an eyedropper.

My mother spent her last months at a Christian Science retreat in San Francisco called Arden Wood. A hotel, basically, with the gospel of Mary Baker Eddy piped into the rooms. Fifteen years after I was told my mom was going to California "on vacation," I found out about Arden Wood, and rented a room there. I walked its eucalyptus-shaded grounds and the hilly streets in the Bay-view neighborhood. I went to the dining room at dusk and sat among aged, infirm guests. That night, in the bathtub, I tried to imagine what it would be like to look down through the water at a body carved by a radical mastectomy, mottled with scars, wasting away. Trying to imagine my mother passing her last painful days without medicine, without family or friends, without hope. My mother was a lifelong Baptist of the deep-rooted Southern variety, born and reared and married and buried by Baptists. She was a church-on-Sunday, church-in-a-church-hat Baptist. Dying in the loveless embrace of Christian Science.

There's an angle.

I'm forty-six now. I've lived with my husband for twenty-three years. Like my mother I had a son first, then a daughter. On my birthday I count my mother's years along with my own. Four more birthdays and I'll be as old as she ever was.

It's common to hear new moms and dads say things like "Now that I'm a parent, I see what my folks had to deal with!" Through ecstatic, sleep-deprived weeks with a newborn, and on into the real work of raising children, fledgling parents often feel the bonds between generations strengthen, renew. Or so I've heard. Motherhood delivered a different perspective to me. Once I was a mom I understood the magnitude of my father's betrayal, the depths of my mother's solitude. I understood that they were not able or willing to put their children's needs before their own—an act I've come to think of as the essence of parenthood.

"Have you forgiven your father?" Before he died I was asked that question now and then. I had different responses through the years but they all add up to the same answer: Not my job. I spent a lot of time trying to figure him out and a lot of energy trying to tell him about me. Then my kids came along, giving me a loving family of my own, and I didn't have much more to say to him. I had tried. Now I could let go.

"Where is your mom?"

When my daughter Lily was three years old she climbed onto my lap one day as I sat at my desk. Lily's middle name is Lady, my mother's maiden name, the signature of my mother's blood. Hanging above my computer were two self-portraits my mother painted in the forties. I had found them in a storage locker in Chicago many years after she'd died.

Lily studied the paintings. Sometimes she knew that the

woman with dark hair and dramatic eyebrows was my mom. Sometimes she thought it was me.

"Where is your mom?" she asked. Her brother Cal, who's four years older, had passed through a stage when that question bubbled up daily. The first time he asked it tears sprang to my eyes, and I couldn't answer right away. Eventually, the question lost its sting.

With Lily in my lap I could almost see the gears working behind her satin brow: You are my mom. Everyone has a mom. Where's yours?

I told my daughter, "She's in my heart."

"Can I kiss your heart?" Lily said. "I want to kiss your mom."

Me too, baby.

And the way up is the way down, the way forward is the
    way back.
You cannot face it steadily, but this thing is sure,
That time is no healer: the patient is no longer here.

T. S. Eliot
"The Dry Salvages"
Four Quartets

Part One

The Way Back

In the first dream my mother sits with me in front of our house, which looms behind us on its fluted columns like a Halloween ghost. We're on the curb where my father parked his cars, our arms cradling our knees, bare feet on black pavement. It's dusk in the dream, a vaporous pause after summer rain. Around us the streets and sidewalks are empty, the large houses and lush yards still.

Since I began to remember my dreams again I've returned many times to the big white house in Evanston. I pass through its rooms like a breeze through a box kite. Asleep I see each piece of furniture, each lost object, in vivid detail. Some nights the house is vacant, as it often was in the last years we lived there. Other nights my sleeping brain animates figures from my childhood, a cast of evanescent best friends and cryptic grownups whose lives are as uncoupled from mine now as the scent of the backyard honeysuckle tree is from its image in a photograph.

This is the first time I've dreamed of my mother.

I can't get a clear reading of her face, just an impression of her pallor, and her sadness. Her bushy black hair is carelessly short, as it was when I knew her. She stares across Forest Avenue and I stare at her. And as I stare at her I begin to notice, or to remember, some of the mysteries of her body.

I notice or remember that her scalp was white and dry and shed flakes my father brushed from her shoulders. The fourth finger of her left hand bent toward her palm, as if warped by the weight of the five thin bands of her wedding ring. One of her toenails was caramel colored, rough as bark.

She sits, squat as a tree stump, pale as marble, and I sit in the same shape, watching her. I want to say *Tell me what happened.* I want to say *Look at me, I'm older now. I can understand. I will try.*

I want to tell her how happy I am to see her but my voice is smoke trapped in my lungs. The damp air muzzles me. In the dream I don't yet know is a dream I reach out to put my arms around my mother.

I bolted upright in bed, torn from sleep, out of breath. I was twenty-nine years old. My mother had been dead for more than half my life.

Bed was a futon on the floor, shared with the man I'd lived with for six years—the future father of my future kids. A Midwesterner, like me. We lived in a rickety clapboard house in Newport Beach, California.

The beach house was divided in two, and we had the front: five hundred square feet of unheated bungalow and a patio the size of an area rug. We slept in a second-story addition slapped together by our landlord, who clearly knew more about cultivating the cannabis flourishing up there when he showed me the place than he knew about construction. Our bedroom—his greenhouse—was made of splintery soft wood, unpainted wallboard and sheets of glass, with a hole cut in the floor for an iron staircase that spiraled to the living room. Through a panel of aluminum windows above our pillows came the drumming sounds of the surf. Through unpainted wallboard at the back of the closet seeped our neighbor's moans when her boyfriend slept over.

I slid to the end of the futon, wrapped my arms around my legs and pressed my eyes into my knees. There she was again, exactly as she'd looked in the dream. Now my mother sat unmoving in the confetti-blizzard blackness behind my eyelids.

There she was. I began to cry, silently at first, then racked with sobs, each gulped breath like a bellows blast on kindling. Startled awake, Kevin came to my side, telling me everything would be okay, don't worry, it's all right, it's okay.

We sat at the foot of the futon as our bedroom-greenhouse brightened. When I'd quieted, Kevin padded down the spiral staircase and returned with tissues, water, cigarettes. I told him I'd dreamed about my mother. Just that. No word pictures, no deconstruction. We smoked in silence.

"Think I woke Steve-Steve?" I said, nodding at the closet. Our housemate's name was Stacy, and as we'd learned shortly after we moved in, her boyfriend was *Steve! Steve!*

"It was time for her to get up anyway," Kevin said.

"But she needs her beauty rest."

"Steve won't mind."

I stubbed out my cigarette. "That was kind of scary."

"Your dream?" Kevin stroked my hair.

"Not the dream," I said, shaking off his hand. "The sound I was making. The sounds coming out of me."

We stared at the tarpaper rooftops outside our gritty windows. The houses in our neck of the Newport peninsula were jammed together like gridlocked commuters. You could hold hands with a neighbor across the narrow passages between million-dollar cottages.

"Very weird sounds," I said.

"Not weird," Kevin said.

"Like some furry animal with its leg in a trap."

"That's all right."

"I was howling."

"It's okay."

"I was baying."

"No, no."

"I was *ululating.*"

Kevin kissed me. "I love when you do . . . that u-lu . . . that you do . . . so well." He stood and held out his hands. "Let's go to Charlie's," he said, helping me up, and we pulled on jeans and sweaters and went downstairs.

I dumped cat food onto paper plates and carried the plates outside. We'd brought our cats with us from Chicago—two pampered, neutered city cats who now had backyards and crawlspaces and miles of fishy sand to explore. Ralph and Rico were waiting for me on the Astroturf patio rug.

"Hi boys," I said, noting a fresh nick on Ralph's ear. I filled their water bowl with the hose, then turned the stream to the potted plants crowding our tiny yard. Since Kevin and I had replaced our landlord's secret garden, these blanched ferns and leggy vines were all that was left of his crops.

Kevin locked the door and we walked single file down the narrow path to the street. The landlord's girlfriend, who lived in the front house on our built-out lot, had left her windows open again. I glanced in as we passed. I could have grabbed her phone from an end table. I could have climbed in. We'd lived at the beach for two years, and most of the habits of my fellow Southern Californians no longer jolted my Midwestern sensibilities. I'd gotten used to the idea of skateboards as the main mode of transport for beach boys pushing thirty. I wasn't surprised to see a woman on the boardwalk seem to speed-age as she approached—looking twenty from a block away but adding years with each step until, passing her, I saw this was someone's aerobicized grandma, with hair the texture of cotton candy and her speckled chest bunched near her collarbones.

But I still wanted to issue warnings like some kind of civilian safety cop when I passed sliding glass doors any journeyman crook could jimmy with a sharp stick, or ground-floor windows steps from the street left uncovered, unlocked, open at night. Didn't anyone read the newspapers? The bad guys came through windows. Children disappeared out sliding glass doors.

We turned right at the sidewalk. The sand was twenty paces ahead. I'd grown up near Lake Michigan, playing in the white lace of lake tides at a beach three blocks from home. When I was old enough to brood I did a lot of it on the rotting pier at Lee Street Beach and the landfill boulders nearby. Now the lake that had whispered through those years echoed in the waves walloping this shore.

Kevin looped his arm with mine as we walked the strand. It was just after six, a dove-gray hour at the beach. We stopped to watch surfers riding the break near the Newport Pier, then I headed into Charlie's Chili while Kevin went to the news boxes. I was sitting in a window booth, peeling blue plastic from *The New York Times* we'd brought from home, when he came in carrying a *Los Angeles Times,* a *USA Today* and an *Orange County Register.* A photo of Ronald Reagan in a Stetson was front page above the fold in all four papers. "Ugh," I said reflexively, at the sight of our Cowboy-in-Chief. Kevin started with *USA Today*'s sports section, and I pulled the features section, called Accent, from the *Orange County Register.*

We'd moved to California two years earlier, in 1985, when I was hired to write for Accent. At my job interview, the features editor said he had openings for a television critic and a "human interest" writer. Which beat did I think I could cover? I told him I didn't watch much TV, so he gave me humans. Some I wrote about were more interesting than others.

One day, after I'd been on the job for a few months, I interviewed a young man who'd survived a car crash that left him with third-degree burns on 95 percent of his body. The staff at the UC Irvine Burn Unit hadn't expected him to live through the night. Yet five years later he was a college student, a soccer player—a "medical miracle," according to his doctors. His name was Tom Handlin, and he was twenty-five when I met him, just a couple years younger than me.

The day of our interview, I headed up the I-5 freeway from the *Register*'s offices in Santa Ana to the apartment in Anaheim where Handlin lived with his parents. He opened the door before I knocked and stuck out a nub-fingered hand for me to shake. I took hold of it and introduced myself.

"Monster!" he said, and smiled. I was getting my first look at a face like none I'd ever seen—a patchwork of rubbery, scabrous skin, pink and gray, white and brown. The eyebrows sewn on in one of more than one hundred operations since the crash were lopsided, the left brow a mere tuft near his temple, the right one a long woolly arch. Our hands parted.

"That's what kids scream when they see me," Handlin said. " *'Monster!'* "

"Kids are monsters," I said, and followed him inside.

We settled at the kitchen table, my tape recorder and notepad between us. I'd come prepared with gentle questions for someone I thought might need conversational midwifery. As it turned out, Handlin barely needed prompts. He was brimming with quick, direct answers—and shtick. A burn unit nurse was voiced in a Monty Python falsetto: "I *am* a nurse! I *am* a nurse! I've gawt a de*gree*!" Describing his pre-crash, post-adolescent self, Handlin drawled like John Wayne. "Don't mahnd me, pardner. I'll just git on mah horse and git out of town."

Of course I was charmed. And the audacity of the charm coming at me, the flame-proof humor issuing from that ruined face, filled me with a kind of wonder that felt almost unprofessional. Any interview worth the time spent has its adversarial moments, even for reporters like me, writing "soft news" features. You have to push toward blunt-edged bits or your story will be as fresh as slept-in clothes. With Tom Handlin, I didn't have to push. Doors flew open before I had a chance to knock.

After we'd talked for about an hour, I made a perfunctory house tour, wherein the Reporter strolls around jotting notes— book titles, memorabilia, a view from a window—while chatting distractedly with the Subject so as not to seem such an obvious snoop. Handlin stopped me as I passed a photo in the living room. It was a formal family portrait, prominently displayed, of two trim parents and their five neatly dressed children.

"Which one do you think is me?" he asked. I studied the faces of the three teenage boys, scrubbed and smiling under gleaming mops of hair. Handlin grew impatient.

"That's me!" he blurted, using a thumb that looked like a cigar stub to point to the boy I'd already decided not to pick—the one any teenage girl would have set her sights on. The handsome devil.

Back on the I-5 a few minutes later, heading south to the *Register,* I knew I'd gotten more than I needed for my thousand-word profile. Toward the end of the interview I'd lobbed a few questions I knew Handlin would like:

So Tom, your doctor said you were burned on 95 percent of your body. Care to comment on what *wasn't* burned?

He raised his one long woolly-worm eyebrow and slyly grinned. "It's like Richard Pryor says, *'Save them! Save them!'* " He fanned his crotch. We both laughed. "My first question was, Are the boys okay? Yeah? All right! Life *is* good."

The *Register's* brand-new Band-Aid-colored offices appeared up ahead on the right. I passed the exit and kept going. In a few minutes the I-5 widened where it joined the 55 freeway. The westbound 55 would take me past a nature preserve in Newport Beach, near where John Wayne's final widow lived in one of his final houses, opening its doors for fundraisers that helped local arts groups and charities—and netted frequent appearances of her tucked-tight, slightly startled features in the society pages. I kept going.

In Irvine I passed low-slung corporate headquarters and clusters of earth-toned stucco houses in master-planned cul-de-sacs. Nearing the Marine Corps air station, I left the freeway at Laguna Canyon Road, a twisty downhill trail through the last of the green hills near the county's shore that hadn't sprouted megahomes and glitzy malls. Ignore the phone poles and overhead cables here and you could imagine western settlers passing through on horseback a century ago. But this was no place to daydream at the wheel—a recent Metro story had named the canyon road, with passing lanes opening and closing in short bursts between sharp turns, the most dangerous in the county.

I was thinking of that story as Donna Summer discoed onto the airwaves.

She works hard for the money . . . So hard for it, honey . . .

Only two years old, the tune seemed to have shrunk, its synthesized keys and tinny drum splashes nagging at Summer's big voice. But it was a decent driving song, and I cranked the radio. A few verses later I was gliding to a stop in Laguna Beach, the lovely, lethal canyon road safely in the rearview mirror. The air was cooler here in town, and carried the scent of the ocean. I passed a row of radically pruned eucalyptus trees, their only remaining foliage clumps of leaves that looked like birds' nests high in the slim white branches. Leave it to sun-struck Southern Californians to trim all the shade from a tree, I was thinking, when I noticed the street sign posted at the intersection: Forest Avenue.

Ten-forty-seven-Forest-Avenue-Evanston-Illinois. That was the address I'd memorized for the first day of kindergarten. It tripped through my brain, dragging a complementary phone number, four-seven-five-five-four-seven-four.

How many phone numbers, how many addresses, had I had since those?

All forgotten.

Donna Summer gave way to Elton John, and I sang along.

Goodbye, Norma Jean . . . though I never . . . knew you at all . . .

I liked this song. I liked this day. I was heading north on Pacific Coast Highway now, the sun-gilded water making me squint behind my sunglasses. The burn-survivor piece would be a breeze—Tom Handlin was a quote machine. And I was on my way home, to be with "mah pardner."

And it seems to me . . . you lived your life . . . like a candle in the wind . . .

Passing Crystal Cove State Beach, I pulled into the turn lane, crossed empty southbound lanes and came to a stop in the cliff-top lot.

And I would have liked to know you . . . but I was just a kid . . .

I flicked the ignition key. The car shuddered and fell silent. "I would have liked to know you," I said, a dull ache in my throat.

What the hell? I must have heard the song a hundred times. I'd never given the lyrics a second thought before.

I looked at the cars parked around me. Their drivers would be down on the beach, walking barefoot by the tide pools, or sunbathing in a secluded spot a short hike north. One of my colleagues, newly divorced, was newly aglow from recent cavorting here with a skateboard-riding beach boy pushing thirty.

I slipped my fingers under my sunglasses and pressed my closed lids. The sun's orange glow bloomed through. You'd never end a piece like this, I thought. If the Subject was going to choke up at the memory of her dead mother, no Reporter worth her column inches would want to set the scene with a pop song. And the ocean at sunset? Please.

Six months before that, in Chicago, my father was waiting for me on North Michigan Avenue. I saw him from the southbound bus I'd caught at Belmont and Sheridan, near my apartment, and glanced at my watch: I was early. He was earlier. He was standing with his shoulders flung back, hands clasped behind him, legs apart—militarily at-ease. Aviator shades tipped to the morning sun. At twenty-six, I'd already given up tanning, though seeing him like that reminded me of sleepy hours we'd spent together on Lee Street Beach, our fingers and toes tickling the sand as we fried.

I got off at the bus stop across from the Playboy Building and jogged across Michigan. After we embraced I stepped back and gawked. "You're wearing jeans," I said. This was news. My son-of-a-tailor father wore tailor-made slacks, linen in summer, wool in winter, each pair worn once and whisked to the dry cleaners. Older pairs were downgraded to weekend use, given away at the first sign of wear.

"Judy got them for me," he said, hiking his belted waistband a notch.

His girlfriend Judy. That figured. "You feelin' groovy?" I asked.

"*Groovy man!*"—the hepcat voice he'd used to mock slang when I was a kid.

So the jeans would be our joke. Good. I looped my arm through his and we went around the corner and into the Westin Hotel.

The young hostess left her podium to greet my father and accept a peck on both cheeks. As we followed her into the dining room she answered his questions about college, about her plans for summer, questions and follow-up questions. I wondered when we'd started meeting here for breakfast on Saturdays. A year ago? Two years? We'd tried weekday lunches, early dinners. Other than a handful of meals at his girlfriend's apartment, where he'd lived for seven years, our relationship consisted of a few restaurant meals every month. We kept the conversation light.

Now here came our waitress slogging toward us, our lifer, swinging pots of coffee and decaf. She was filling my cup when my father began ordering—eggs scrambled *dry,* bacon *crisp,* white toast *buttered and hot.* She had to set the coffee pots on the table to get out her pad. When she looked at me I wanted to apologize. I ordered quickly and let her get away from us.

"I read your article in *Playboy,*" my father said, smiling at me over a vase of daisies. "I've shown it to a few people and they were very impressed. John H. Johnson, for one. And John knows a little bit about writing."

Johnson, the publisher of *Ebony* magazine, had been a client of my father's ad agency many years ago. His name still came up often, with a kind of reverence, though I didn't know how much contact they had anymore.

"That was quite a coup, wasn't it?" he said. "Writing an article for *Playboy?*"

"It's just a little profile," I said. "The music editor's a friend."

"Well, dear, he gave you the assignment. And I assume he was pleased with your work."

"She."

"Pardon me?"

"The music editor's a woman."

"I stand corrected."

"But you're right," I said. "You're right. It's a good byline for me. I'm glad to have the clip."

My father stirred his tea. I'd been a secretary at *Playboy*—that was where Kevin and I had met in 1981, four years ago. The editor I typed and filed for had let me write what's called "house copy," which is text that appears without a writer's name attached. Gobs of house copy were needed each month, I learned. Soon other editors were giving me unbylined blurbs to write, and paying me *Playboy*'s generous freelance rate. When payments for my contributions exceeded my secretarial paycheck, I decided to quit. At our next restaurant meal together, I'd told my father my plans. He advised me to keep my job. *Playboy* was a good company, he'd said. A good solid company. I was living with Kevin now, he'd pointed out, but what if we split? What would I do then?

Our breakfast arrived. I put out my cigarette. "So I have some biggish news," I said.

"Well, I guess 'biggish' news is better than 'little-ish' news," my father said.

"I don't know if you remember—I went to L.A. a few months ago."

"I have a very good memory, dear."

"Right. Well, one of the papers I interviewed with offered me a job."

My father's fork halted en route to his mouth.

"It's called the *Orange County Register,*" I said. "The features editor called yesterday. I guess I'm going to take the job."

Huge smile. "That's marvelous! Just *marvelous.*"

"It's good."

"This is a whole new chapter for you, dear."

"I guess."

"This is very exciting," he said. "But what about Kevin?"

"He's quitting."

"I see."

"Not right away," I said. "There's a trial period. I'm being hired on a three-month trial. I guess if I'm acquitted I get the job."

"And when does this trial period begin, may I ask?"

"Soon. I'm going in a few weeks."

He reached across the table for my hand. There was emotion in his eyes, the whites clouded blue. "I'm going to miss our Saturday morning routine," he said.

"Me too," I said, wondering if I would.

He paid with a credit card. I watched him sign his girlfriend's name. When we were back out on the street he said, "Take a little walk with me," and I looped my arm through his as we started south on Michigan, passing the sunken plaza in front of the Hancock Building. I glanced down at the café tables in the little courtyard, wondering if the architect could have known that a single-story hole in the pavement would drain your attention from the black behemoth rising from it. Or was that the plan?

"I have a little news of my own this morning," my father said, and fished a business card from his wallet.

"Nice," I said, running a finger over the raised letters. I tried to remember what that printing process was called—was it embossing? We'd played this scene many times before. Card stock and print style were things he cared about.

"It's kind of a funny story," he said, and began to tell me about his new client, the one listed on his new business card. Since my father went bankrupt eight years ago, he'd been working freelance from his girlfriend's apartment, or from office space loaned or rented to him by the owners of small ad agencies like the one he'd had. I never knew the specifics of his business arrangements, or if he made any money from his work. But he was always proud of his new calling cards. There was one he'd had printed when he got a perfume account, another for that chain of suburban hair salons, one for the crazy vitamin lady . . .

"Here we are," he said, as we reached the brown marble arch of Neiman Marcus. He held the door for me, and as we entered the bright retail space my father's features seemed to smooth out, his body relax. He loved luxury. Tucking his sunglasses into his shirt pocket, he went straight to a jewelry counter in the maze of display cases. The saleswoman greeted him by name.

"This is my daughter Pamela," my father announced. I was hanging back. He gestured for me to come closer.

"Pamela is a journalist," he said, "and this morning she told me of a wonderful new opportunity for her in California."

"Congratulations!" The saleswoman's smile raised brackets of wrinkles.

"Thanks," I said.

"But California! So far away from your family!"

My father had moved around the display case. "Now, ladies," he said, *"s'il vous plaît! Vôtre attention ici maintenant!"*

And I remembered the game we played when I was a kid: *S'il vous plaît* was "silver plate." *Ce n'est pas important:* Snapper's important. I dug for another phrase, recalling him, for an instant, as he'd been when we played our word game: dancing toward his dresser in undershirt and boxers, arms out, fingers snapping, mugging at the mirror. *"Parlez-vous français?"* he'd say. *"Chev-ro-lay coo-pay!"* I'd answer, and burrow deeper in the still-warm sheets on my mom's side of the bed.

My father was examining a bauble in the saleswoman's hand. "It's really a fun piece," she said. "Everyone loves it. *Loves* it."

I drifted toward them. Now he was holding the thing, a watch. His thumb circled the red enamel band framing its face. The saleswoman put a little velvet cushion on the counter and placed other enamel bands on it. Green, blue, yellow, black. She took the watch, snapped off the red band and replaced it with the green one.

"Isn't that *fun?*" she said, handing it back to him. He held the watch under a pinstripe of light. Then he looked at me and smiled.

"What do *you* think, beautiful daughter?"

"Um . . . I . . . it's nice," I said. Nice idea, anyway. I'd never wear it, but it was nice of him to buy me a going-away present, or congratulations present—however he thought of it. I put my arm on his shoulders and kissed his cheek.

"Judy just loves this kind of stuff," he told the saleswoman. "She probably has ten watches in that collection of hers—"

"She'll love this one," the saleswoman said, snapping another band in place. "*Trust* me."

"All right, I'll trust you! Wrap it up!" my father said, and they laughed.

Wool tongue, tastes like something died on it. Black knife at the temples, ice-edged. And cold, *cold,* digging my feet into the seams—

Till a biker ripped down Rogers Avenue. I opened my eyes.

Day. Okay. Sticky skyline of empties on the coffee table. Ashes everywhere, like new snow.

"Laura?" I said.

I was twenty-two years old. This was the fifth place I'd lived since my father went bankrupt four years ago. I pulled my feet from the couch seams and sat up. One of Laura's hammered-silver bangles was stuck in the coffee table sludge. I tried her new name. "Lee?"

Gone, I thought. Whoever you are. I went into the bathroom for aspirin and got the hell out of there. At the kitchen sink, mouth to tap, I let the hiss and bubbles and metal flavor flow through, carry the dead out.

Waiting for the steel-drummer hammering on my head to go on break.

Watching the red dial sweep seconds from the oven clock.

It was nine-fifteen. So I was fucked.

I turned off the tap and called Melora at the temp agency, reading her number from a Post-it stuck to the wall by the phone. When she answered I croaked a greeting. "I'm sick as a dog," I said. Half-true.

"Where are you?"

I could hear phones ringing all around her. I could see her ferret face. "Home," I said.

"Nine-thirty Monday morning you're telling me you're sick."

"I just woke up."

She cut the line. Okay. As I hung up I noticed the bruise on the back of my hand. I scraped off a freckle of dried blood, made a fist and looked inside my elbow: thick vein bulging in there now. Ha. Where was that blue river last night?

I showered and dressed and went back into the bathroom to scrub blood stains from the sink and tile, following driplines from bathroom to kitchen, kitchen to couch. Rust-colored Pollock-splotches of a rank amateur: me.

Not like Laura-now-Lee, my attending physician. Laura-Lee with her bag of tricks. Laura'd gone pro.

What did she think when I opened my door last night? What did she see?

I saw a cowgirl in Frye boots and leather-fringed jacket— ninety pounds of tan and bones, ninety-five with her silver and turquoise. Same costume she'd assembled when we were class- mates at Nichols Junior High. When we were best friends.

Laura had appeared at my door last night ten minutes after she called. And I'd felt embarrassed. Her eyes darted around my unloved rooms. Her Fryes tapped across the bare floor as she buzzily recounted her day. As if days were what separated us.

"My mom made me play *tennis*," she groaned, dropping onto the couch. She was home for the holidays. I pictured her in her parents' house in Evanston, a mile north of here. She'd had a pink bedroom three times the size of mine on Forest Av- enue.

"I tried everything I could think of to get out of going to the club," she said. "I'm *tired*. I'm *sick*. I've got *jet lag*. But you know my mom."

I set bottles and glasses on the coffee table and sat on a pillow on the floor across from her. "Does she still wear that hairpiece- bun thing?"

"Ha. You remember that."

"I remember one time we were messing around with her make-up and I reached into a drawer and touched one of them. Scared the shit out of me. I thought it was a little animal curled up in there."

In sixth grade we'd talked about horses and given ourselves Bonne Bell cheeks and Maybelline eyes at the vanity in Laura's frilly bedroom. In seventh we played guitar duets. *"I caught you knockin' at my cellar door . . ."*—trying to sound as bedraggled as Neil Young. We were into the liquor cabinet by eighth grade, up on the roof with a Baggie, Zig Zags and a Zippo. In high school we lost touch.

Now she lived in Arizona. Now she had a new name. Why find me now? Why bother?

I asked about tennis. Laura looked at me with one side of her mouth curled—half a smile. Half of something. "I had to make my excuses and go buy a turtleneck first," she said.

And when I said I didn't understand she put her beer down, popped the pearl-backed snaps on her cuffs and rolled up her sleeves. I looked at the brown lines on her sun-toasted skin. Called tracks because they led from one point of entry to another, I guessed. And for their color, maybe—like weathered rail ties. Laura's were.

When I finished cleaning I put the burnt spoon and spent needles from last night into a garbage bag with the bloodied towel I'd used to mop the bathroom, put that bag inside another and took it out with me—fumbling with gloves in the dark stairwell, twisting a scarf around my neck and up over my face, tugging my hat to my lashes. No matter. The wind sliced through my mummy wrap the moment I opened the door. Blade-to-the-bone wind. Arctic mother*fuck*. I started down Rogers bent to the lake blasts. I was thinking of the liquor store on the corner of Rogers and Sheridan, next to Biddy Mulligan's.

I was thinking I'd dump the bag there, between a liquor store and a blues bar. Closer to Juneway Jungle, the white-girl no-fly zone on Juneway Terrace, than to my landlord, who lived in a little house behind his building, his porch windows staring at the tenants' trash cans.

Dump the bag, call Melora again. That was the plan. Melora had sent me out on three jobs in a row, had given me two months' solid work. The temp agency was busy. And I was *good* at this, I thought, rehearsing my plea. I'm perfect for anonymous temp work. I type fast, I can handle the phones. And I don't want to know *them* any more than they want to know *me*. I'm a girl in a beige suit, passing through.

This was a blip. We'd fix it this morning. Unless Melora put it together with drinks last week. There was no connection but she might make a connection. But what was I supposed to say? She said an after-work drink, a holiday drink. What was I supposed to say? "Okay, *but I'm not gay!*"

Two blocks down Rogers I turned around and started back. Biddy's was too far away. My fingers were Popsicles. The stale smell of spit and damp wool gagged me inside my scarf. I jogged past my building, the wind at my back now, pushing me along. At the top of the hill I crossed Ridge Avenue and glanced north. A mile north was Evanston, where Laura was probably still sleeping. Or maybe her mom had taken her to the tennis club again, where we used to sit in the steamy whirlpool, and bake on the sauna's cedar planks. I tossed my bag in a trash can on the corner. Crossing back, I saw Armand in the window of his grocery store. A moment later I pushed through the store's fogged door.

"Hello miss," he said, rubbing his hands together, sharing the cold with me. He was wearing a knit cap pulled down to his thick brows. "How are you today? You like coffee? I give you coffee."

"That would be great. Thanks." I stuffed my gloves in my pockets and took the styrofoam cup he offered. As I took a sip I noticed him looking at the storm-cloud bruise on my hand.

"What's it say about the weather?" I asked.

"No good," he said, his gaze shifting to the *Trib* spread open by the register. He read aloud, tracking the words with his finger. " 'The temperature dropped to a new low for the season, nine below zero, early Sunday.' "

"A 'new low' last night," I said. "That's almost funny."

"Not funny, miss." He looked up from the paper. "People are freezing. Old people are freezing, every kind of people."

"No, no, I didn't mean the weather was funny. Sorry. I was thinking about something else."

The crease at the bridge of Armand's long nose deepened. He returned to the newspaper, moving his finger as he silently read a story under the headline MEXICAN TIE FORGED BY PRESIDENT-ELECT REAGAN. There was a picture of grinning Reagan handing some grinning guy a shotgun.

"I was going to ask a favor," I said. Armand didn't look up. I took a sip of coffee and tried again. "I'm getting a paycheck on Friday, but I'm a little low till then."

Armand's finger held his place as he met my gaze.

"I was wondering if I could write you a check and date it Friday," I said.

"Can't do it, miss."

I thought *Why? We've done this twice before.* But maybe that was why. "Just for fifty," I said.

"Sorry, miss."

"You know I'm good for it, Armand."

"I don't have it," he said, holding both hands up, as if this were a stickup.

"Okay," I said, and put my cup down. "Thanks anyway. Thanks for the coffee."

I turned, putting on my gloves, as the fogged door swung open. An older woman maneuvered a baby carriage over the tread. Armand greeted her, offered her coffee. I looked under the stroller's hood at a postcard of chafed flesh framed by blankets, the little mouth clamped on a mitten. The baby rolled its watery gaze to me.

It was 1978. I'd just turned twenty. I was counting my take in a back booth when Frank ushered out the last philosopher. Bruno was replaying his highlight tape for the two cops who came in as Frank locked up.

"You see that flicker of *holy shit!* at the last second . . . ," Bruno said. He'd come around the bar a couple hours ago to toss some poor jamoch on his ass—*bounce!* Now he set out two porcelain mugs and poured single-malt whiskey. Anybody passing by on Lincoln Avenue would see that two policemen had stopped into the 2350 Pub for coffee.

". . . little pussy's going *You can't touch me! Don't fuckin touch me! I'll call the cops!*" Bruno said. The cops liked that.

I finished counting and pulled two bills from the pile. The new busboy was doing Kara's sidework. I went over and handed him a ten.

"Gracias," I said. I didn't remember his name. He took the money looking at his splattered boots and went back to refilling ketchups.

"Why you no eat tonight, Marin?"—*mah-reen.* My common-in-Spanish name. Ramon was grinning gold through the kitchen service window. I put the other ten in the check rack and spun it. "Stomach ache, amigo."

The cook crushed one nostril with a blunt finger and sniffed hard through the other.

"Funny," I said.

"You too skeeny." He rolled a toothpick around in his mouth.

"Las mujeres flacas son las mejores en la cama," I said, a line stolen

from a lifer I'd worked with at the Water Tower Hyatt. Skinny women are better in bed.

"Aaaaiiiee!" Ramon howled, his voice blending in with the others now joining Bruno's at the bar. The crew from the Barleycorn was rolling in—that waitress who always wore tight white jeans, the bartender who looked like Cat Stevens, a couple more I didn't recognize. All shouting. Here to drink free and overtip. The Barleycorn and a few other bars on the block closed at 2:00 A.M. on weekends. We closed at 4:00. In the hours between those two types of liquor licenses, sometimes till dawn shut down the party, a lot of hard-earned dollars passed among the help.

I took my tray of tips to the bar and waited for Bruno to cash me out.

"I heard Stallone's in it," someone said. Talking about a movie that was going to be shot on the block, the big news for weeks. The movie people had been hanging around Katzenjammers, across from the Barleycorn.

"James Caan." Frank jangled his keys. "It's gonna be Jimmy Caan."

Kara clip-clopped up from the basement bathroom wafting peppermint, her honey mane puffed with fresh brushstrokes, lips reglossed. She'd busied herself long enough for the busboy to finish her sidework. One of the cops whistled through his teeth as she slid onto a barstool.

Kara was the head waitress, Frank had told me after a cursory glance at my job application. We'd been sitting in a back booth. If I was going to work here, he'd said, I had to try not to fuck with Kara. Did I understand? "Yes." Did I have a problem with that? "No problem." The pay was a buck an hour plus tips. "No problem," I'd said. On my application I'd left the space for age blank, and he hadn't asked, so we both knew how old I wasn't.

The wolf-whistle cop lit Kara's cigarette as Bruno poured her a shot of Schnapps. Then Bruno reached for another bottle. "You in?" he said, tilting a single-malt at me. A guy I didn't recognize glanced over and said, "She new?" Bruno shook his head.

"She looks new."

"Now, now," Kara said. "She's a good little newbie, a quiet little newbie, and we don't want to scare her away."

"She don't look scared."

The whiskey was a lit fuse, throwing sparks as it went down. My stomach cringed. "I gotta go," I told Bruno, and he took my stacks of coin and small bills and turned them into seven twenties. I handed him one.

"Thank you, ma'am," he said, bowing, then Frank unlocked the front door and I was out.

Warm night. Steady traffic on Lincoln Avenue. Stragglers caucusing by parked cars. I jogged to the corner, pressing a hand to the knot in my middle, dropped back to a walk on Belden Street. Townhouses lined both sides of Belden east of Lincoln. It was darker here, but I could hear my footsteps on the pavement. I'd know if someone was coming up behind me before he got close.

I looked into the sleeping homes, wondering which one I'd take if I could have my pick. On the other side of Geneva Terrace the homes mixed in with three- and four-story apartment buildings. My building was on the next corner, a brick box with a dry cleaners' neon scribble in the first-floor windows and a brightly lit white-tile entrance. The decorative front door, with its heavy glass panes and arched top, reminded me of a church window. I unlocked the street door, pulled trash from my mailbox, unlocked the inside door and walked up three flights of rubber-lined linoleum.

Feeling nauseous. Feeling relieved. My next shift was Wednesday, and Wednesdays were slow. And it was three days away. By then I'd be fine.

My apartment was a room with a strip of a kitchen on the back wall and three windows up front. I dropped my clothes on the sofabed in the middle of the brown carpeting and took a long bath. Dressed in a robe, I raised the nylon window shades the previous tenant had left behind and sat at the desk I'd made from book boxes shoved under the windows. The lady who lived in the townhouse across Cleveland Avenue poked her disheveled head out her front door and picked up her Sunday paper. If I had my choice of homes on that block I'd take hers. And all those lovely bookshelves in her front room, too.

I rolled a sheet of paper into the typewriter I'd bought with last month's spare twenties and opened *Typing for Beginners.* I was on Lesson 11, Finger Drills.

"All through the night the trains hurry along the river," I typed.

"Have them join you tonight in the room above the store."

"The prize was awarded to the zealous and excited pupil."

"Try to do your typing with a smooth and an even rhythm."

My Smith-Corona hummed as the room brightened. After a Capital Letter Drill I brought a frozen cheesecake to the desk and paged ahead in the typing book, poking at the dessert's thawing edge with a fork from the 2350 Pub. I cleared a moat that tasted more like the tinfoil container than cheesecake, then put my fingers back in position for a Punctuation Drill.

"Here is the bill," I typed. "It is hers. Give it to me. It is not mine. Ask her for it. Please do it now. This is the one."

When the door buzzer sounded my hands flew off the keys. I'd lost track of time. I jumped up and pulled on the rank jeans and T-shirt I'd left on the couch, buzzing my father in without bothering with the intercom. He was stopping by before church, as promised.

"Hi," I called down, wondering if I should change clothes. We'd probably go to the Belden Deli for breakfast. He liked the onion rolls there.

My first glimpse of him in the dark stairwell was a gray fedora, then the broad-shouldered silhouette in a black suit. When he got to my floor I saw the envelope in his hand. He came to me and kissed me on both cheeks, handed me the envelope, turned around.

"Thanks," I said, as his striped usher's pants flicked past the railing, his quick steps carrying him down. One hand rose above the fedora to wave goodbye.

Back in my room I opened the envelope. Five fifties, straight from the bank. He liked new money. I tucked the starchy bills into my wallet. Five fifties would cover the abortion I'd booked for tomorrow.

H elen?"
  "Pammie!"

"Hey girl." I climbed onto the kitchen counter, stretching the phone cord taut. I'd just gotten back from freshman year at Hampshire College. It was May 1977.

"I was wondering when you were coming home," Helen said. "I called a couple times but no one answered."

"Ain't no-bod-y home," I sang, one of the tunes in our tiny repertoire. Once last year we'd hauled our Gibsons to Rogers Park for open-mike night at the No Exit Cafe. The sound of Helen's bell-like soprano amplified at my side had nearly given me lockjaw.

"I'm only here a few days," I said.

"Well, damn. Where're you going?"

"Baah-ston."

"You're going back to school?"

"No, I'm just going to get some crappy job and hang," I said. "A guy from Hampshire got us a place. He's from there."

"Pammie."

"It's not what you think."

"Well what *is* it then?"

I looked out the window at the side yard, where my mom had built a rock garden. "It's a brotherly-sisterly thang," I said. "I don't want to be here this summer."

The rock garden wasn't a garden anymore, just a forgotten corner of scraggly shrubs and dirt patches where my mom used to plant perennials. She'd spent a summer when I was seven or eight arranging boulders around a reflecting pool, then laying flat stones in a curved path between the pool and a cedar bench under the kitchen window. But we'd never really used the area as she must have hoped. The water in the reflecting pool drew mosquitoes, and the bench, in deep shade, was damp with dew most of the day. If you wanted to sit in our yard you'd go to the picnic table on the patio, where we used to eat in warm weather, or stretch out on a lawn chair under the honeysuckle tree.

"What are you doing now?" Helen asked. "Want to come over?"

"I'll call you back," I said, and slid off the counter to hang up the phone.

Pushing through the kitchen's swinging door to the dining room, I saluted the statue of one of the biblical Wise Men, an old habit. Our Wise Man stood on a pedestal fitted into the corner behind the piano, one hand to his crown, the other reaching out as if to give his gift. My parents had bought him in France.

I crossed the library and stood at the front door. The glass top of the door was open. I curled my fingers on the iron grillwork. The glass foyer doors, the front porch columns and the evergreens standing sentinel at the edge of our yard symmetrically framed a picture that made no sense. Hadn't made sense when I'd stood here before I called Helen, didn't now. My dad's gray Benz was parked at the curb with my brother in the driver's seat. My dad was in the passenger seat, crying.

A hunchbacked pack of cyclists sped north on Forest Avenue. I thought about my ten-speed Raleigh, awaiting me in Boston. If my father would buy me a plane ticket I'd leave today. I heard the shouts and sandal-slaps of kids running down Greenleaf Street, headed to the beach. I watched them dash between the cars on Forest. If my brother would drive me to the airport I'd go now.

My brother lit a cigarette. My father wiped his face with a white handkerchief.

We'd gone to the Pancake House in Wilmette for breakfast. I'd expected a lot of questions about school—neither my father nor my brother had ever been to Hampshire College—so I'd brought pictures along, thinking I'd give a photo tour over pancakes. Pictures of the condolike dorm I'd lived in with six students, of the wooded horizon surrounding campus and the quaint town nearby, Northampton, Mass. I'd brought a picture of the friend who'd rented an apartment in Boston. I was going to tell my dad about my summer plans.

But as soon as we'd ordered, they started talking about work. My brother had dropped out of Tulane University two years ago to work for my dad in a new business they called "the phone company." He had an office across the hall from my dad's agency, stacked with boxes of phones with calculators built into them. And he . . . what? Sold the phones? Dealt with production so my dad could sell them? Standing at the front door, I tried to recall what little I knew about the phone business, and what had been said at breakfast that might have upset my father.

After a few minutes I went back to the kitchen, hiked onto the counter and stuck my feet in the sink under the window. I turned on the tap. Our maid Frankie washed clothes by hand here. My mom had cleaned her brushes here, and stirred gallons of house paint custom-mixed at Good's on Main Street. The porcelain still held scars from her handiwork—the pale gray she'd used on the back steps, forest green from the front porch, the bubblegum pink I'd chosen for my bedroom when my brother moved to the attic. Turquoise.

The kitchen door swung open and my brother walked in. He stood by the stove, an unlit cigarette in his hand. He looked out the window over the sink. Then his eyes locked on mine.

"What . . . ?"

"Dad's going bankrupt," he said.

"*What?*"

"Dad's going bankrupt. *We're* going bankrupt."

"Wait—is this about the phone company? 'Cause I know you guys—"

"This is triple bankruptcy, Pamela—"

"—were talking about it—"

"Listen. Just *listen.* A lot of shit went down when you were gone. So here's the deal, okay? He's losing the agency. He's losing the phone company. And he's taking personal bankruptcy." My brother ticked off the losses on his fingers. "One, two, three—got it? Triple bankruptcy. Do you understand? The house is gone, the car's gone. And you can forget about going back to your stupid little college. That's done. Do you understand what I'm saying? Why the fuck are you laughing, you little twit? Are you fucking stoned? *What the fuck is wrong with you?*"

Frankie was still here. I kicked off my boots in the foyer and hurried to the kitchen. She was at the stove, stirring right, snapping left. Her scratchy voice matched the radio singer's note for note.

"If you ever get the notion . . . You-oo miss me too . . . Just make it in a hurry . . ."

"Hi!"

She spun around. "Girl! Don't sneak up on me like that."

"Sorry."

"You're home early."

"I ditched French."

Frankie dipped a hand into the front pocket of her workdress and turned down the volume on her transistor. Then she shot me a look.

"It doesn't matter," I said, going to her side. The skillet held a pepper-speckled slush of peas and potatoes and pearl onions—my favorite. "I don't see why I even go to school anymore."

"I'm not hearing that."

"I got early acceptance at Hampshire. I'm *in*. Who cares about high school?"

"I do." She put her arm around me and stuck her nose in my hair. "Whatchoo been smokin'?"

"What*choo* been smokin'?"

"Don't be fresh."

"Sorry."

"It's a nasty habit," she said, handing me the wooden spoon. I went up on tiptoes to kiss her before she stepped away.

I peeked in the oven at a pot roast simmering with carrots and potatoes. My dad and I would eat the roast and the peppery peas for dinner tonight, and I'd have three or four more dinners from the leftovers. I liked Frankie's food better than the stuff he bought at the deli. And now that my brother was away at Tulane, the meal she cooked every Friday lasted me half the week.

"You got a letter from your grandmother," Frankie said, settling on the big barstool at the end of the counter. She put a match to a Carlton menthol and picked up her pencil. On the counter in front of her was a quarter-folded section of newspaper. I glanced over as she touched the pencil nib to her tongue and filled in a line of blanks on the crossword puzzle. She took a long draw on her Carlton. Dragon smoke streamed from her nose.

I wished we could be friends, like my mom was friends with her. I wanted to sit with Frankie at the counter, like they used to, drinking coffee for hours, eating bacon sandwiches.

"You could read the letter if you want," I said.

"It's for you, baby."

"I know, but she always asks about you. We could read it together. And then we could write her back together."

Frankie tapped the puzzle with her pencil. " 'The Bridge of San *blank* Rey,' " she read.

"Luis."

"It's only got four letters."

"No *o*," I said. "L-u-i-s."

"The Bridge of San Luis Rey," she said, filling blanks. She took another pull on her Carlton.

"My dad likes that book a lot," I said. "He gave me his copy from, like, college or something."

"Ooo baby that reminds me—your daddy called a little while ago. He said tell you he has plans tonight."

The song had ended and a voice was jabbering in Frankie's pocket. She reached in and switched off the radio.

"I could eat this whole thing," I said, stirring.

"Did you hear me?"

"He has plans tonight."

"That's right."

"I'm starving."

"You need to turn the oven off at five. And take that meat out and cover it."

"Okay."

"Don't you burn up my beautiful roast now."

"What if I do?"

"I'll beat your what-if-I-do butt!" she said, and reached out to swat me with the newspaper on her way to the bathroom. My mom had rigged a closet for her in the little bathroom by the back stairs. Behind a curtain that covered the space under the steps, Frankie stored the blue workdresses and canvas shoes she wore while she vacuumed and dusted our house, washed and folded our laundry, ironed a week's worth of my dad's white handkerchiefs and boxers.

When she'd changed back into her slacks and knit top she opened the bathroom door. I turned to watch as she put on salmon-colored lipstick and combed the curls that framed her face. Frankie was six feet tall and shaped like a Y—broad shoulders and a huge chest tapering to narrow hips and pipe-stem legs. Her ass was as flat as my dad's.

"Can I drive you to Howard Street?" I asked. She was pouring lotion into her palm, rubbing her hands together.

"All right," she said, flicking the bathroom light with her wrist. "Take that fry pan off the fire and let's get to gettin'."

We went out the front and down the walk to my brother's car—mine this year. He wasn't allowed to take it with him to New Orleans. I started the car, eased to the corner and turned right on Greenleaf, then right again onto Sheridan Road. It would have been quicker to take Chicago Avenue, but Frankie didn't say anything about my route.

I wanted to drive her all the way home. I wanted to see what her house looked like. I thought of where she lived as *the ghetto,* though I knew not to use that word around her. Frankie had worked for my parents when they lived in Chicago, and once she told me that she would have quit when they moved to Evanston but she didn't because she loved my mom. She had a husband but no kids. Right after my mom died she came to our house every day and sat with my grandmother, playing Chinese checkers and watching *As the World Turns* and listening to Billy Graham on the radio. After my grandmother's brother came to take his sister away, Frankie went back to once a week.

I parked on Howard, across from the el.

"You make sure to write to your grandmother," Frankie said.

"Yes ma'am."

She hoisted herself from the bucket seat and shut the door. "All right," she said, tapping the roof. "I'm gone."

At home I went straight to the kitchen and turned off the oven. The roast could finish cooking while the oven cooled. Even if it didn't, at least I wouldn't burn down the house.

I carried a bowl of peppery peas up the back stairs to my grandmother's bedroom and closed the door. This spring it would be three years since Uncle Doc took my grandmother to live in a nursing home near his house, in Greeneville, Tennessee. She'd left all her furniture behind, all her kitchen stuff, her books about religion, cooking, gardening, the South. Little by little I'd moved into her rooms. Now I slept in her bed, showered in her bathroom, read on the couches in her sitting room and did my homework in the pink kitchen my father called "Nellie's Diner." Her Singer sewing machine was still in there, near the window where she'd grown African violets.

I pulled the chain on the bedside lamp and leaned the envelope addressed to me against the lamp's pink ceramic belly. Whoever had written this one—nurse, aide, candy striper—hadn't even bothered to add "Nellie Lady" to the return address.

I ate my bowl of peas, then opened the letter.

Dear Pamela, I read. *The weather is very beautiful here today, although the temperature dropped into the low twenties last night. I am enjoying these sunny days—*

I tossed it aside. Why did they do that? Did they think I wouldn't know? I reached into the dresser's top drawer and dropped three fat buds in a rolling paper. My grandmother's plastic drawer dividers still held her sewing needles and spools of thread, postage and Green Stamps, clip-on earrings and bits of costume jewelry, coins, rubber bands, ribbon. The drawer used to smell like her face powder. Now it smelled like pot. I lit up and held the sweet smoke down as long as I could, exhaling through my nose like a dragon. I watched the girl in the mirror. When her joint was a roach she dropped it in the soup bowl and stuck her hands in the dresser. Behind the plastic drawer dividers— more envelopes. Dozens more. I sifted through until I found one postmarked May 18, 1974. A year and a half ago. One of the last letters my grandmother wrote for herself.

Dear Pamela,
I am thinking of you tonight. I do not like to write since I do not make a very good job of writing anymore. I would like to know about your riding and your music. How are you doing in your guitar lessons? Do you get to church? I know I am missing a lot not being able to be with you as you grow up. I feel that I have let you down. I hope you will come visit me. I am not going to try to write a long letter. My hands are so bad I will have to stop for a while. I love you very much.
Grandmother

I turned off the lamp and climbed under the covers. When I woke I lay in the silver light, listening. When I was younger, lying in bed in my pink room, I'd watched for what felt like hours every night as stripes of light rolled across the ceiling— headlights on the cars on Forest Avenue. When a northbound car passed a southbound car in front of our house the ceiling stripes splashed together for a moment, making a white diamond right over my bed.

I thought a voice had pulled me from sleep but now I didn't hear it. I got out of my grandmother's bed and went to her door. The top flight of our front stairs was carpeted, to cover treads that tripped a burglar alarm we hadn't used in years. The carpet muffled my footsteps. Below the landing the bare wood crackled. And startled my dad and his date. When I reached the library he had gotten up. The redhead on the big blue couch was buttoning her blouse. Her hair covered her face but I recognized her. She was the cashier at the hardware store.

My mother was falling, and I looked away.

I saw she was falling, looked away, then pretended to notice all of a sudden. Trying to replace what I'd seen with a new moment of noticing, with this action-I-was-taking—trotting into the middle, *ho!*, jumping off.

You don't jump off a horse when it's this cold. Even beginners know that. You slide down. You ease down.

Helluva Note snorted, like he was saying *What are you doing?* We'd just started. Holding the reins, I hobbled a few steps on stinging feet.

By then my dad had helped my mom up. He was brushing her off. He'd taken off one of his gloves and he was brushing her pea-coat with it. The dirt in the indoor ring isn't like regular dirt, it's soft and sticky, like powdery snow. Dry-sticky. It was all over the front of her coat.

"Are you okay?" I asked.

My mom was looking at the ground. The bit jangled in Helluva Note's mouth.

"I think that will be quite enough for today," my dad said—furious.

What did I do?

He smacked his glove on his leg to knock the dirt off and Helluva Note shied from the motion of his arm, the crackle of leather. By the time I'd calmed my horse, my parents were at the gate. They went into the barn and disappeared down the middle aisle, where Helluva Note's stall is. I led my horse over and closed the gate, then got back on and let him trot.

The wind was banging on the metal door at the other end of the ring. Helluva Note's ears were pricked to it. I cut through the middle, passing close to the cinder blocks the instructors stand on and the tall swivel chair lying in the dirt. I pressed my outside leg against my horse, trying to get him to bend, to listen to me. He bulged out of the turn and broke into a canter. I pulled him back to a trot and circled again.

My dad knows better than to leave the gate open when someone's in the ring. He used to ride polo ponies when he was at the University of Chicago, or maybe it was before that, when he was in Milwaukee Country Day School, with rich kids. He's the one who started me riding in the first place. On my sixth birthday he took me to Coach House Stables but they said, "Come back when she's seven." I think I cried. I don't remember what happened exactly—it's a long time ago. I'm fourteen now. I took lessons at Coach House for a couple of years, then we switched to here, Peebles' Stables, I think because it's closer. When we switched stables my dad started riding again. In good weather he takes a school horse named Handsome out on the trails through Harms Woods.

Helluva Note kept breaking into a canter, so I let him go. He had to get his ya-yas out. My dad bought him for me last summer. He's a ten-year-old bay gelding and a total sweetie. My dad paid Mr. Peebles fifteen hundred dollars and we got the papers that show Helluva Notes's bloodlines, which is how he got his name. His dam was Helen Highwater. I can't remember his sire's name. I wanted to keep the bloodline papers in my room but my dad said we should put them in the safe deposit box with the money for my college education.

My mom went *"ah."* That's why I looked over. She was sitting in the tall swivel chair Mr. Peebles sits in when he teaches and the chair was falling and her hands came out of her coat pockets and she said *"ah."* I looked away before she hit the ground.

I was surprised she wanted to come with us this morning. She's not a morning person, like me and my dad. Maybe she wanted to do something special because it's New Year's Day, or because she's going to California tomorrow and she won't see me ride for a while.

I pulled Helluva Note back to a walk and loosened the reins. That would have to be it for today. My dad was probably freaking out that I was taking so long. I walked my horse until he cooled off, then led him back through the barn to the cross ties, put my saddle and bridle in the tack room, fastened his blanket and took him to his stall. I was saying goodbye to him when I noticed my mom at the stall door. I slid it open for her. Helluva Note came right over.

He put his nose to her collar and licked her neck near her ear. He doesn't do that to me. He isn't interested in anyone else's neck, just my mom's. I think he likes her perfume. Maybe it tastes good. His tongue is as thick as my wrist.

She grabbed the fat hook that holds the water bucket and for a second I thought she was going to fall again. I think she's tired. That's why she's going to California. When my horse licks her neck I'm always a little scared he'll nip her but he never does. She closes her eyes. It's dark in here but I can see her teeth when she smiles.

W e bought the house for Pamela's second birthday," my father said. He jiggled his hand, swirling the wine in his glass. I took a sip of ice water from a glass shaped like his, holding my glass the way he does, by its stem. This is the long boring part of Sunday lunch when we have guests and I have to stay at the table even though I'm done. That's why there's wine, too.

I crossed my legs so I could see my new shoes in the mirror. My mom wanted me to get round-toe shoes again but she let me get the ones I wanted. The salesman kind of helped me out. He'd already measured my foot on the metal thing and then he went over and stood by the shelf that has one of every kind of kid's shoe on it and pretended he wasn't listening to us. I was holding the shoe I'd taken from the shelf and my mom was holding the one she'd taken. I told her round-toe shoes were too babyish for junior high. She said pointy shoes would squish my toes together and my feet wouldn't grow right. But I can't wear babyish round-toe shoes to sixth grade, I said. I *can't*. That's when the salesman came over and said maybe I could pick shoes from the other side next time. He pointed behind us, where there's a shelf with one of every kind of grownup's shoe on it. He said I'd probably fit into the smallest size of ladies' shoes by next year. I guess my mom got the hint.

My new shoes are white boots that come up to my ankles, with zippers on the inside and little swirls and paisleys made from dots in the leather. I bounced my leg, watching my white shoe-boot in the dining room mirror. The mirror fills the wall between the windows behind my dad. I can see bits of everyone at the table in it.

My dad swirled his wine. Now he was starting the story about buying our house. The wine is called Vouvray and it's French, like our guests, Georges and Michelle. Georges is a graduate student at Northwestern University and he comes to our house for Sunday lunch. I'm not sure how we met him but if I had to guess I would say that my dad called Northwestern one day and asked if they had a French student who wanted to get to know an American family. Like if he was lonely or something. My dad might have said that his dad, Jacob Marin, was from Alsace-Lorraine. My grandfather Jacob Marin died before I was born but my dad talks about him a lot, and he showed me where Alsace-Lorraine is on a map. He told me about the French and Germans fighting for it. Jacob Marin came from the French side. I guess that's why we like France and French people, because we're part French.

Every time Georges is here my dad asks a bunch of questions about Pompidou and Charles de Gaulle, and they talk about the French government. My dad throws in sentences in French and says *"alors"* and *"ah, oui"* a lot. *"Votre amie est très jolie!"* he said today, and he kissed Michelle on both cheeks, like the French do. Georges has brought some of his French friends over for lunch but Michelle is the first girl, so she must be his girlfriend. She's French too, and pretty, with long black hair and blue eye shadow, but she's got really strong b.o. When she hugged me, I almost puked.

The story about buying the house is mostly about my mom. I like it better than the ones my dad tells about when she worked at his advertising agency. When he talks about those days he says how much fun they had, and what a great art director my mom was, with great ideas for logos and ad campaigns. I like all that.

But somewhere in there he always says she had a twenty-seven-inch waist back then, and he puts his hands out holding on to twenty-seven inches of air. When he does that my mom looks down at her lap.

When he tells the house story she watches him the whole time. She can sit so still.

Before they bought our house they lived on Elm Street in Chicago. They rode the bus down Michigan Avenue to 624 South Michigan, where my dad's agency is, and when it was nice out they walked home, window-shopping and talking about logos and ad campaigns. Then my brother was born and then I was born and then my grandmother came up from Tennessee to live with us on Elm Street and help take care of me and my brother. That's when my parents decided to move to the suburbs, my dad said. In the mirror behind him I see my mom put her hand on top of my grandmother's hand. She leans over and says something only my grandmother can hear.

My mom started scouting the North Shore for a house, looking and looking for months and months, but she didn't want to buy any of the houses she saw. Then one day she saw our house and that was it. She just knew this would be our house. She knocked on the door and a little old lady opened it and they stood on the porch talking and talking but the little old lady didn't ask her to come in, even though there was a For Sale sign on the lawn. The little old lady was standing in her doorway like the inside of her house was a big secret.

My father stopped talking. He scooted his chair back a little. You could see he wanted to find a nice way to say the next part, he didn't want to say anything mean, but he had to finish his story. Everyone was waiting. He looked up at the ceiling, then he looked around the table. The little old lady finally let my mom come in, "and it was *godawful*," he said, and everyone kind of laughed. He told about the dark wallpaper and the heavy drapes and the thick carpeting inside the little old lady's house, and I know what he means. We have white walls and white see-through curtains and shiny wooden floors. Our dining room furniture is the color of chocolate milk. There's a tea table by the windows and a big chest called a sideboard across from me, with another big mirror and little wooden cherubs on the wall. My mom had a carpenter build a pedestal that fits into the corner behind the piano, and she put a statue of one of the Wise Men from the Bible up there. He's chocolate-colored, too. He's a little shorter than me.

My dad made an offer on the house "and here's the kicker," he said, like he always does. Then he told how the little old lady already had a bunch of offers, and all the offers were for more money than my parents could pay, but she liked my mom so much she wanted her to have the house.

That was in 1960, just in time for my second birthday.

"Heckuva birthday present, eh kid?" he said, turning to me. My mom and my grandmother and Georges and Michelle were looking at me, too. They were all smiling. I touched the hem of the lace tablecloth my grandmother made.

"May I please be excused?" I said.

"*Certainement!*" my dad said, and everyone laughed.

The back stairs creaked as I went up. I stopped by the window near the top and looked at the monastery across from our house. The monastery was a gray stone castle, with turrets and church windows and a fence that looked like it was made of black spears. You could walk on the stone base of the fence, hanging on to the spears, even if there were monks working in the yard. They never said a word. They wore long robes with rope belts and in the summer you could see their sandals poking out from under the robes.

The blind monk was standing on the corner now, his red-tipped cane tapping at the curb. When he'd crossed Forest Avenue I went up to my room.

I opened my closet and checked my shoe-boots one more time, then changed from my church clothes into shorts and a T-shirt. I went to the railing by the front steps and listened. Georges was telling a story, and the kitchen door was swinging open and shut. They would have dessert, then coffee. That would take a while. I went into my parents' room, next door to mine.

My mom painted the walls and ceiling turquoise in here. Some mornings I slip into her side of the bed when she goes downstairs for coffee. I lie there, in the still-warm place she left, while my dad shaves at the marble sink in his shaving room. He whistles through his teeth while he shaves, then he steps onto a machine that looks like a parking meter with a canvas belt attached to its sides. The belt looks like a girth strap. I know all the parts of the saddle, all the parts of the bridle, most of the parts of a horse. I've been taking riding lessons for four years. When I'm a little older my dad is going to buy me a horse.

Every morning my dad puts that canvas belt around his middle and turns a knob on a machine that makes the belt shake, jiggling the loose skin on his furry stomach and back. After he jiggles for a while he puts on goggles and sits on a footstool in his boxers with his face tipped up to the blue light of his sunlamp. He only tans his front, same as when we go the beach. His front is the color of cooked bacon. I guess he doesn't mind that his front and back don't match.

A big laugh comes up from the dining room. I pass my parents' bed and go into their closet. They keep their clothes in a narrow room that separates their bedroom from the bathroom I share with them. My mom painted all three rooms the same deep shade of turquoise. At the far end of the closet is a bookshelf that holds my mom's shoes and handbags. I choose a pair of pumps from the messy stacks, slip in my feet and clump back to the mirror near the door. My feet are almost as big as my mom's but my legs are much thinner. Much better, I think, studying them in the mirror. I unzip my cut-offs and let them fall, stomping my high-heeled feet free. I turn to see myself in profile. There's the bump of my pubic bone, a jutting chin. I lift the elastic band and look at the little beard coming in. It's a concern. Yesterday I opened the bathroom door just as my mom was getting out of bed. Through the open closet doors I watched as her nightgown caught in the froth of sheets and blankets. It rose onto her stomach, baring a black triangle reaching up greedily from between her legs. Would my soft moss grow tangled and weedy like that?

I put her shoes back, trailing a hand through her blouses and dresses and skirts. At the mirror again, I check the line across my back, barely visible under my T-shirt. I've studied that line many times in my own closet mirror. There isn't much to see up front but I need a bra now that I'm in junior high. All the girls in my class have bras this year.

My mom bought her dresser unfinished and painted it to match the rooms. I know before I touch the painted knobs that they'll feel gritty. I know the drawer will squeak as it slides open.

There they are, four of them. I pick one up. The cups are huge. I can't imagine the tender buds I cover with the flat triangles of my training bra ever swelling to fill cups like this. *Over-the-shoulder-boulder-holder* the boys at school shout, laughing. They slap each other's shirt fronts. *Chest eyes!*

The right cup of my mom's bra could hold a grapefruit. The left cup is full. I bring it to my face, muzzling my nose and mouth with its cotton padding. I press it against my eyes. I remember seeing my mom standing here last week with her hands busy in the turquoise dresser. I remember how I felt as

I watched her from the green-blue shadows beside her bed and I realize now that it was my movement—my stepping toward her—that set her hands aflutter. I heard the squeak of bare wood sliding against its like. I saw my mom's chin sweep around like a sail tugged by a gust. "Sweetheart!" she said. "You surprised me." When she turned to me her hands were empty as seashells.

Part Two

The Way Forward

The long hallway again. Tall windowless walls. Unmarked doors spaced along the walls. All the doors are closed.

I walk to the end of the hall and turn right. I'm in another passageway exactly like the last one. It goes on like that for a while, right or left at each dead end, left or right, it doesn't matter. I follow my feet through the maze. When I reach her door this part of the dream is over.

Sometimes the halls have the too-bright look of a hospital. Once I hurried along catching glimpses of a man in a lab coat leading a woman in a hospital gown by what seemed to be a leash. I rounded each corner just in time to see them disappear around the next—his coattails billowing, her bare feet shuffling, the black strap taut between them. I pulled myself up from that one in a sweat.

Other times the hallways are styled like a hotel's, softened with fabrics and lighting designed to muffle and soothe. The hotel setting induces a different kind of panic. In the hospital I clatter down the halls to find the patient—to see what's been done to her, and to help her if I can. In the hotel I'm an interloper, an unannounced and possibly unwanted guest. I make my sluggish way on the spongy carpet, my thoughts sinking with each step. She came here on her own. She wants to be here, alone. This is where she went when she went away.

Her door is never locked. When I open it I find her sitting in an armchair by a window that frames bright green leaves flecked with sunlight. Her eyes are trained on the branches. Her hands lie in her lap. She turns to me.

A nn's on the phone," Kevin said. He stood in the open screen door of our rental in Newport Beach, holding the receiver.

I shot him a black look. That he'd brought the phone with him—that Ann could probably hear us—meant I had to take the call. Had to get off my ass and work, or at least think about work. Stop brooding for a minute.

As I knew was happening too often lately, my anger struck the least-deserving target. "Goddamn it," I mumbled, avoiding Kevin's gaze as I took the phone.

I sat back down next to Ralph, our cat, who promptly rolled into a patch of sunlight on the Astroturf patio rug and began to purr. Of our two cats, Ralph was the lover, eager for any strokes he could get. Tiger-striped Rico was probably up the alley somewhere stalking a seagull, or getting his ears chewed by a tomcat. I picked up a flea comb and dragged it through Ralph's fur.

"Hey Ann," I said into the phone as brightly as I could. "What's up?"

Ann Conway was a friend from the *Orange County Register,* where she was the paper's society writer and the features staff's honorary grownup—a mother of five with a decade or two on the rest of us reporters. Tall and curvy, with inky bottle-black hair and theatrical make-up, she was the kind of woman whose emphatic womanliness made me feel like my own femininity fit in the spectrum somewhere between preteen boy and dyke. But I liked Ann. We were both early-bird writers, often the first reporters logging on at the *Register.* One morning before sunup I walked into the bathroom at work and found Ann at the sinks in spiked heels and a form-flattering knit dress. The outfit was routine for Ann. Her long nails were freshly glossed bright red. The surprise was her bare face: Without make-up she looked years younger, and I told her so. "You don't need all that," I said, pointing to the pots and pencils she was laying out by the mirror.

"That's sweet, honey," she said, cocking a naked eyebrow at me, "but if I went out looking like this, they'd call the paramedics."

I'd quit the *Register* after only eighteen months—about as long as I'd lasted as a secretary at *Playboy,* and more time than I'd served at any of the restaurants and bars where I'd been a waitress. Newsroom work had taught me how to write on a deadline measured in hours, rather than a freelancer's days or weeks. Daily interviewing had sharpened those skills. And I'd written some pieces I was proud of: the profile of burn survivor Tom Handlin; a multipart feature about a surrogate mom; a Sunday story about a dusty bar in Ensenada where Orange County's pampered young people emptied their wallets, drinking till they puked.

But the better I got at the mechanics of the job, the more I chafed at the work. When knocking out a weekly feature became routine, I knew my days on the "human interest" beat were numbered. I wasn't interested anymore. I missed the fervor I'd felt when I was a secretary trying to figure out how to be a writer, drafting outlines and rewriting sentences until I knew them by heart—all for a few twenties and a byline in the free *Chicago Reader.* When I quit the *Register* I'd hoped to dig into a story that would scare me again. Instead, I'd drifted into the journalistic equivalent of stringing beads.

Ann Conway had quit around the time I did, and moved up the food chain to the *Los Angeles Times.* She'd started sending me to cover Orange County society events, and those assignments had led to two other weekly features at the *Times*—a column called "Single Life" and a cooking column called "Galleys" that included recipes. Fundraisers, lonely hearts, recipes: I was up to my elbows in hack work, and for a while that had suited me fine.

Not anymore. In the months since my mother debuted in my dreams, sitting with me outside our house in Evanston, she had returned in dozens more, each dream throwing a longer shadow over the days that followed. I was weepy half the time, angry the rest. I wouldn't have lasted a day amid the jangling phones and chattering voices of a newsroom. And now I was having trouble putting on a game face for my freelance hack work.

I left Ralph and his fleas, carrying the phone inside so I could jot notes as Ann gave me my assignment.

"I'm there," I told her when she'd finished.

"You're a peach," she said. "Are you writing in the morning?"

"I thought I would."

"I'll leave my office open for you. Use my computer. And look in my top drawer, will you, sweetie?" Ann said. "There's a note in there for you."

"A love note? Do I have a secret admirer?"

"Have a look. It's no biggie."

"I want a biggie. I want a secret admirer with a biggie."

"Go to work."

"Yes, ma'am."

"Kiss to Kevin."

"That's easy."

"Be a good girl," Ann said.

"Not so easy."

We said goodbye and I walked from the office to the spiral staircase in the living room. "Kevin?" I knew he wasn't up there. You couldn't hide in our half-a-shack.

He must have slipped out while I was on the phone. Didn't want to be cooped up with me. Couldn't stand to hear my voice. I wanted to tell him that I was sick of me, too.

I carried my notes up to my desk and dropped them on the files by the typewriter. The top file was tabbed "Panic." I knew I should dump it in the trash, but I wasn't done brooding about it yet. While I was with the *Register* I'd interviewed a psychologist who wanted to write a book about panic attacks. As every reporter soon discovers, half the people you interview want to write books. They have *amazing* stories to tell, *fantastic* ideas for books—all they need is someone to put their pearls on paper. They seem to think that the only thing separating them from their own shelves in Barnes & Noble is stenography. One woman I was interviewing about single parenthood slipped into a screed on her ex-in-laws' furniture business, how her ex sold coke from the warehouse, carted it around inside sofas, blah-blah—a charming tale boldly told as her five-year-old played with dolls at our feet. "I'm going to write a book about that sonuvabitch!" she said. "Will you write it?"

I turned down that one, but I'd agreed to write a book with the shrink who pitched panic. Call him Dr. Blauhardt. We'd had a handshake deal while I spent hours interviewing him in the evenings after work, then I had hired a lawyer to make our agreement official. I wrote a book proposal, got an agent—and the agent scored a ten thousand dollar advance. We were waiting for contracts from the publisher when Blauhardt backed out of the deal.

The file below Blauhardt's bore the name of an aging starlet. After the panic doc panicked, the agent who'd made the deal asked me to meet with a woman who'd been the personal assistant of a seventies TV icon I'll call Fluffy. The assistant wanted to spill. Could I see if she had enough dirt for a tell-all book?

Off I'd gone in my red Tercel to a ranch house in the San Fernando Valley, where Fluffy's former flunky lived with her two young children and a crew-cut husband who came on like a drill sergeant. "What makes you think you can write this book?" he demanded, moments after I touched down on their chintz-covered couch. "You've never written a book! We don't know anything about you!"

After the Sarge buzzed off, his nervous wife and I got to work.

For the next few days I interviewed Nervous, transcribing my tapes at night in a motel nearby. She'd been in the inner circle through the early years of Fluffy's tumultuous romance with another waning star, and for a while after their love child was born. Nervous had seen and heard plenty, and even had a big scene of her own: Unpacking after a flight to London, she said, she'd opened a suitcase Fluffy had asked her to carry through customs and found a diaper packed with cocaine and marijuana. Tears! Fears! Two weeks' notice!

I'd written a book proposal, but so far the agent hadn't scored.

I flipped open my 1988 Week-At-a-Glance and turned to my freelance tally. In January, I'd had thirteen assignments from the *Times:* three society pieces for Ann (at $225 per), five singles columns ($350 per) and five cooking columns ($150 apiece). So I'd made $3,175 last month for writing I didn't even bother to read when I sat with my *Times* in Charlie's Chili. I added the assignment Ann had just given me to the February list, then dug out a sheet of paper I'd tucked away early this morning. Before dawn I'd pulled the page from my typewriter and stuck it between my files, facedown, unread.

Who was I hiding it from?

M in the hotel room. I go in and I'm hardly looking at her. I go over and lie down on the bed and I'm looking at the ceiling and it's the ceiling over my bed in Evanston. I'm saying How was I supposed to know? How was I supposed to deal with this? More questions like that. I'm looking at the ceiling and not even looking at her but what I feel coming from her is total surprise. I'm losing what happened exactly, I don't think she talked at all, I just got waves of feeling from her that were total total surprise. Maybe a touch of resentment. Maybe a touch of laughing at me.

"Hey," Kevin said. He was on the spiral staircase, a few feet from my desk. His normal speaking voice is soft and he'd lowered it further so he wouldn't startle me. We tried not to sneak up on each other when we were working.

I wasn't working. I was staring at the chicken scratches of a hastily transcribed dream. I wiped my eyes with my shirttail. Kevin reached through the bars of the staircase railing and placed a box of tissues on the carpet between us.

"Dr. Kleenex to the rescue," I said.

"Do you have a soc tonight?"

Soc—pronounced "sock"—was short for "society," meaning Ann Conway's assignments: the soc beat. "Yup," I answered. "In fucking Anaheim."

"I'll drive you."

"You don't have to."

"I want to."

"Okay." I plucked a tissue from the box. "It's a date."

He started back downstairs.

"Kevin?"

He turned. "Pamela?"

"I don't know what's going on."

"I know."

We got off the I-5 on Katella Avenue, heading due west in a February sunset strong enough to burn skin. I reached up and pulled down my sun visor, then flipped down Kevin's. Ahead was the Alamo Inn, with its neon covered wagon, and the Alpine Motel, bivouacked below the snow-capped peaks of Disneyland's Matterhorn. It was cocktail hour. Soon families drawn to Uncle Walt's acres would drag back to their discount lodgings, as businessmen and loners cruised for amusements of their own. As any diligent reader of the Metro pages knew, the land around the Magic Kingdom was Hooker World.

We crossed Harbor Boulevard and slid into the shadows of the Anaheim Convention Center. Kevin braked in front of the Hilton but I didn't want to get out of the car, didn't want to work yet, so I rode with him to the self-park lot beyond the valets' domain. I was in my soc uniform: black dress, black sheers, black pumps. I'd bought the dress and shoes for the first party Ann sent me to and had worn my dressed-up journo duds to every soc I'd covered since. Sometime during the past year, after the twentieth fundraiser, or the thirtieth, it had become a point of pride for me that I hadn't popped by the Dress Barn for a second outfit. My plain wrapper was a sandwich board: "I'm Not Like You."

"This should be quick," I told Kevin as we walked into the hotel. He'd brought along a FedEx sack stuffed with magazines and newspaper clippings about high school girls' basketball in Iowa—research for an assignment from *Sports Illustrated.* An editor he'd worked with at *Playboy* was now at *SI,* tossing Kevin freelance plums.

He pointed to the sack. "No rush."

I stepped onto the long escalator leading up through the three-story atrium. Riding backward, I blew a kiss and watched as Kevin did a little shuffle-dance for me. Then I turned, with my private smile, to take my first look at the soc.

Gowned women and men in dark suits filled the landing outside the ballroom. The men laid their hands on one another's backs and looked around for a waiter toting champagne. You could see their boredom from fifty paces. As the escalator carried me up I picked out half a dozen women I knew from other soc-beat parties. The aging poster girls of salon and spa, making midlife careers of doling out their time and their husbands' cash. I took out my notebook and went to the check-in table.

"We're so glad to see you!" said the volunteer who handed me a press kit. We both knew she'd be happier if Ann Conway were here—for the status Ann's presence would confer, and the better play the party would get in the *Times*. But she was savvy enough to flatter the stringer.

"Thanks," I said, and scooted off before I had to say more. I matched the names Ann had given me on the phone with the list in the kit, then set out to bag some quotes. Forty minutes later, my notebook pages bearing lifeless quotes and names double-checked for spelling, I was leading the chairwoman and a few others to an ice sculpture crowning the dessert buffet. I stood with the *Times* photographer as he got his shots, then I left, collecting Kevin from the lobby bar on my way out.

Back outside in the cooling air I felt almost giddy. Now the only thing separating me from my $225 freelance check was a small stack of paragraphs.

"The chairwoman said, 'mental blot,' " I told Kevin as we zoomed south on the I-5. "She couldn't remember something because she had a 'mental blot.' "

"That's worse than writer's clamp," he said.

"Now *that* would have to go in the paper. I don't know about 'mental blot,' though."

"She said it."

"I know, it's tempting. But it might be mean."

"Mean, or satisfying?"

"Both," I said. "Like me. Hey, let's go by the *Times*. Ann left something for me in her office. She was very mysterious about it."

The *Times* housed its large Orange County bureau in a tan shirt box of a building, with newsroom windows overlooking an empty field near the South Coast Plaza mall. I flashed my *Times* ID at the security guard, who raised the guardrail to let us in. Kevin waited in the car as I jogged through the sliding glass front doors and clicked across the lobby in my sensible heels. Ann's office was unlocked, as promised. I dropped into her swivel chair and opened the drawer under her keyboard. On top of her pens lay an envelope with my name on it. I pulled out the papers inside.

The first page was a letter to the paper's top editor in Orange County.

"An acquaintance . . . recently commented negatively about one Pamela Marin," the letter writer, whose name I didn't recognize, began. "He was trying to be constructive."

He mentioned a soc I'd covered for Ann, "where OC business people socialize with the consular corps. The complaint was that Marin, who was seated at the table of the chief of protocol . . . was inappropriately dressed and she stood out in a negative way—to the detriment of The Times image . . . The story she wrote . . . ignored positive spins . . ."

Clipped to the letter was a computer printout of my story. Ann must have gone into the *Times* archives and made a copy. Or maybe the top editor did. I read the lead:

> Following established protocol for snappy speechify-
> ing, master of ceremonies Erich Vollmer anchored his

podium duties at the "International Protocol Ball" on Saturday with an anecdote.

Lightly overwritten, I thought, and read on.

Facing nearly 400 guests at the Four Seasons Hotel in Newport Beach—among them 42 consuls general from the Los Angeles consular corps and local business heavy-weights—Vollmer told a story about Franklin Delano Roosevelt, who reportedly hated social events.

Vollmer, executive director of the Orange County Philharmonic Society, beseeched the evening's honorary chairman, James Roosevelt, not to tattle if this particular tale from his legendary father's life was a fable.

Jesus, I'd written "tattle"? And *"beseeched"*?

According to Vollmer, F.D.R. so hated the superficiality of high society occasions that he took to greeting people by saying, "I murdered my grandmother today." To which they simply smiled and made polite and inattentive responses.

"Except for one time," said Vollmer, when the President used his line on "a lady who was actually listening. She said, 'Well, I'm sure she had it coming to her.' "

Fact or fiction, that was one of the few moments of levity during a pre-dinner ceremony that was less than the hosts had hoped for.

Or, as event chairwoman . . . said as she stood outside the ballroom in the middle of the muddle: "This is terrible. I want to go home and disappear."

Ha. Sometimes a right-place, right-time quote falls into your notebook. Then you get paid for stenography.

I left the newsroom scanning the last of my hack-work report. At the bottom of the printout was the caption that had run under the picture with my story—names of the guests I'd chosen to pose that night for the *Times* photographer.

I flipped back to the letter. The writer's "acquaintance"—the whiner who was too much of a wuss to send his own letter to the editor—was the husband of the chairwoman who'd called her own party *terrible.*

"That was quick," Kevin said when I opened the passenger door. He looked at the envelope in my hand. "What's in there?"

"Fan mail."

He started the car.

"A guy from a soc wrote to say he liked my dress," I said.

"He better watch out."

"No, he wrote to say he liked my personality."

"He had definitely better watch out."

"Especially—how'd he put it? My 'positive spin.' "

We pulled out of the parking lot, turned left onto Harbor Boulevard and headed south, toward Newport Beach. In knotted traffic under the 405 I took off my pantyhose and tossed them in the backseat. Then I reached for Kevin's hand.

"Next stop margaritas?" he said.

"*Sí.*"

He glanced over. "You okay?"

Traffic loosened once we were out from under the freeway ramps, and now we were zipping down Harbor's bright corridor of car lots, passing showroom windows painted with exclamation points as tall as upended trucks. Rows of new cars shone under strung balloons.

"I was thinking about when I was nineteen," I said. "Nineteen or twenty."

"I wish I'd been there."

"I'm glad you weren't. It's actually kind of weird to me that it was only ten years ago." I looked out the window. "I was working at this place called Kelly's. It was on Webster, right under the tracks. It's probably still there. Near Raoul's—did we ever go there? The Mex place?"

"I don't think so."

"I know we didn't go to Kelly's," I said. "It was a gross job. College kids ordering pitchers of beer, shit tips. I only worked there a couple months. The owners were this superfat couple—the wife fussed around in the kitchen, the husband fussed around at the bar. He was so huge his stomach rubbed against the speedrail."

"There's an image."

"Anyway, one night this drunk DePaul fuck said something to me, and I said something back. And he said, 'What would your *mother* say if she heard you talk like that?' I said, 'She's dead.' And he said, 'Well what would your *father* say?' And I said, 'He's dead.' "

Kevin squeezed my hand.

"There was this thing I used to say, around that time, at nineteen, twenty. I'd kind of forgotten about it, but it's back now. If somehow it came up in conversation that my mom had died, and someone said, 'What did she die of?' I'd say, 'Bone cancer.' I can hear myself saying that. And I remember when I would say it, as I was hearing the words coming out of my mouth, I was thinking, *Did she?* It wasn't like I was lying, it was like— guessing. Like I didn't know. But I kind of knew that some part of my brain had written that in: My mother died of bone cancer."

"Poor Pamela."

"It's not 'poor Pamela,' " I said, and instantly regretted my sharp tone. "Sorry."

"It's okay. This is hard."

"And what *is* it, anyway? What's going on? I keep thinking about her and dreaming about her and crying about her—but it's not really about *her*. It can't be, because I don't know her. I don't know who she was."

Harbor emptied into Newport Boulevard. We passed Kinko's, Denny's, Dippity Donuts—three of our late-night haunts.

"I have to do something," I said.

"What do you want to do?"

"First I want to stop doing this." I flung a black pump over my shoulder. It smacked the vinyl backseat, landing near my wadded pantyhose. "Do you know I'm making more now than I did on staff at the *Register*?"

"You're doing well."

"I'm writing crap," I said, and tossed the other shoe. "I'm sick of it."

Downhill on Newport Boulevard, we crossed PCH and sped onto the peninsula. Now the road was flat. The Newport peninsula, as the local papers noted in their evergreen earthquake stories, was mostly sand. When the Big One came, this hangnail on the county's coast, crammed with surfers and idle rich, would basically melt. The term was "liquefaction."

Kevin pulled up beside El Ranchito and cut the engine. A thumping beat from the restaurant's jukebox filled the car. Neither of us made a move to get out.

"I want to go to Tennessee," I said.

"Okay."

"She was born in Kingsport."

"The Mets have a minor-league team there."

I looked at Kevin. "That's what I thought."

"About the Mets?"

"About Kingsport," I said, watching a couple push through Ranchito's door. "That's the first time I've ever said the word 'Kingsport' to you. We've been together for six years, every day, every night, forty-five conversations a day—and I've never said 'Kingsport.' Because if I had, you would have said that line about the Mets, and you never said that line before. I would have remembered it. And, you know—or you don't know, how could you?—I went to Kingsport with my mom every summer."

Kevin touched my face. "I want you to do whatever you want to do. Okay? I'm for it."

"I want to go to Tennessee and dive in. Start where she started and follow it through. I need to find out what her life was."

"I think that's right."

"She died 'when I was a kid'—that's what I always say. *When I was a kid.* But I was fourteen when she died, you know? Shouldn't I know who she was if I had fourteen years with her?"

"I don't know."

"Shouldn't I have a fucking clue who the fuck she was?"

The jukebox paused between songs. I reached into the backseat for my shoes. "Sorry," I said, my anger spent. Misspent. "But shouldn't I?"

"I don't know," Kevin said, opening his door. "You were a kid."

Two weeks later Kevin was in Iowa reporting on girls' basketball and I was planning my return to Tennessee.

I told Ann Conway I needed a break from the soc beat, and thanked my other editor at the *Times* for all those checks for all those columns about Orange County's singles and home cooks. I was done with hack work and on to the big scary story I'd been waiting for. The one waiting for me.

I booked a flight to Tri-Cities Airport—Bristol, Johnson City and Kingsport gave it its name. That triggered memories of heading south with my family twenty years before. My father drove us six hundred-and-some miles from Evanston to the eastern tip of the state, zeroing out the odometer as we pulled away from our house so that when we arrived he could report the exact number of miles we'd traveled. The number would quickly dissolve into another number indelibly written in my young mind—624 South Michigan Avenue, the address of his office in the Loop, where the marble wall outside his door held a brass plaque that looked as permanent as the lions outside the Art Institute: ALLAN MARIN & ASSOCIATES, ADVERTISING.

At the wheel of one of the Cadillacs we had when I was in grade school, or one of the Lincolns that followed in later years, my father kept his grip at ten and two. "Toot-toot-tootsie goodbye-eye!" he'd sing, as the miles passed under our car like a string of accomplishments.

My grandmother sat in the back with me and my brother, her hands busy with a crochet needle and a patch of lace. The silken thread trailed down to a black patent-leather purse at her crossed ankles. Every now and then she flattened the lace flower against her leg and tugged the thread to loosen the line. When my brother and I burst out in laughter or argument she turned to the window, the scenery scrolling across her stop-sign-shaped glasses. "Goodnight *nurse,*" she'd whisper, looking wounded, as if our voices had struck her like blows.

My mother sat in front with my father.

Remembering, I closed my eyes and listened. My father whistling through his teeth as he drives. *"Fermez la bouche!"* he snaps, eyeing his noisy children in the rearview mirror. My mother turns and smiles at me. I *make* her smile in my daydream, but I can't make her talk. I've lost her voice.

When we got to Kingsport, we checked into the Downtowner Motel. For the next few days I raced up and down the steps from the balcony outside our rooms to the courtyard pool. I knew we were staying at the Downtowner so my mom could get together with Dorothy Hale, her best friend growing up, and my grand-mother could get together with a bunch of old ladies whose names I couldn't keep straight. Dorothy lived in town with her husband Roy and a son named Jim, who came to the motel in his swimsuit. Jim and my brother and I spent hours taking cannon-ball leaps into the deep end and eating lunch by the pool in our dripping suits.

A few days after we got to Kingsport, we'd repack and move to a farm outside town. "The Farm"—shorthand for the whole vaca-tion—belonged to my Uncle Riley and Aunt Lily, who were about my grandmother's age, and a woman about my mother's age named Juanita, who had come to live with Riley and Lily as a child and never left.

Riley and Lily Hite. My grandmother was Nellie White. She'd married Henry Lady and had one child—Mildred Elizabeth Lady. My mom.

I knew my mother's parents both came from big families with deep roots in eastern Tennessee, though I couldn't say how the

Hites fit in with the Ladys and Whites. Framed photos of my grandmother's siblings had hung in the hallway by her rooms in our house in Evanston. Stern-faced country people, posed in horseshoe-shaped groups, squinting in the sun. I wondered what had happened to those pictures. If I found them, how many of my aunts and uncles could I name?

My father drove us to the Farm and returned home alone, leaving his wife and kids and mother-in-law for a month in the country. For a suburban kid like me, every day on the Farm was an adventure. I tagged along with Uncle Riley when he brought the cows down from the hillside pasture to the milking barn. I crawled into the feathered air of the chicken coop to gather eggs for Aunt Lily. I rode a tractor through tobacco fields, and bloodied my knuckles on blackberry brambles, and sat with Juanita on the back porch popping the ends off green beans until my chatter or the mess I was making brought a gentle swat—"Git!"—that let me know I might be family but I was still a tourist here, a little Yankee mascot with a funny accent and the lean dark looks of my city-bred father.

On a hillside near the farm was a white clapboard church with a steeple that reached beyond the treetops. My mom and I walked down the gravel driveway, past a pond rimmed with plants that smelled like onions and stalks of Queen Anne's lace taller than me, scuffing our Keds in the dust at the side of the road. She led me through the fronds of a willow and up to the churchyard gate, then wandered by herself among the graves, kneeling to touch the letters and numbers cut in granite, scraping moss from flat stones buried in long grass. I climbed onto the tallest monuments and leapt off.

After my mother died, we stopped going to Kingsport.

After she died, Uncle Doc took his sister—my grandmother—back to Tennessee. When had my grandmother died? I remembered visiting her once in my teens, flying down from Chicago alone and staying in Greeneville with Doc and his wife Mabel. I

sat in my grandmother's room at the nursing home, reading to
her from the Bible, as she'd asked. She called out my mother's
name when she saw me, repeating it throughout my visit. *"Mildred,"* she whimpered, reaching for me with a hand that looked
like it was made of twigs and mottled leaves bundled with blue
yarn—a child's treasure brought in from the woods. *"Help me,
Mildred."*

I pushed away that memory and went to the phone. The
Kingsport operator gave me Dorothy Hale's number, and
Dorothy answered her phone on my first try.

"Well I declare," she said when I told her I was coming to
town.

My flight from LAX stopped in Charlotte, where I had a short
layover before catching a commuter plane to Tri-Cities. The walls
of the Charlotte airport bathroom held a single graffito: "I love
God because he loves me too! (Forever no matter what!!!)" Wher-
ever the Mason-Dixon Line was, I thought, I must be south of it
now.

At an empty bank of phones I called the hotel in Des Moines
where Kevin was staying and recorded a short message on his
room's phone service. I lit a cigarette and called back.

"Tomorrow's her birthday," I said. "Sixty-five." The tape
recorded dead air to its beep. I redialed.

"It seems kind of bad-fiction dramatic that this is the timing,"
I said. "I don't know if I did this on purpose, or if it just happened. She was coming at me. Now I'm going to her."

I took a long pull of smoke. "She died on March 12. Buried on
the Ides. I think about it every year but I never said anything because—" *Beep.* Never mind.

Back onboard I reached into the seat pocket for my book. "We
are talking now of summer evenings in Knoxville, Tennessee," I
read, "in the time that I lived there so successfully disguised to

myself as a child." I flipped through the worn pages of *A Death in the Family,* looking for a half-remembered passage, a scene with Rufus, the little boy who learns of his father's death, sitting in the chair where his father used to sit, running a finger through the dust on it, tasting the dust—

Never mind. I put James Agee's lovely sentences away and pulled out my notebook, jotting back through the morning, from the Bible thumper's bathroom scrawl to the cabbie's patter on my trip to LAX.

"John Collins," I wrote. The driver and I'd had a laugh at the rube he overheard trying to order a Tom Collins last night. Then I wrote, "I was a bartender in Chicago." I'd said that to the cabbie. Why?

I stared at the sentence. I had been a waitress—in bars—in Chicago. Why the résumé upgrade? To impress the alkie driving me to the airport?

I knew I'd said it before. "I was a bartender . . ." "When I was a bartender . . ."

She's dead. He's dead.

Bone cancer.

I watched the plane's wing cut through cotton. The "why" questions would have to wait. Right now it was enough just to hear myself taffy-pulling facts, and quit doing it. Or what was the point of the trip?

Crossing the tarmac at Tri-Cities, the heat pressing on me, ironing me, I scanned the hilly farmland surrounding the airport's unfenced perimeter. I felt like I'd flown back in time. Up the metal steps to the gate and there was Dorothy—a still-trim, steel-haired woman in her sixties, neatly turned out in navy slacks and a red blouse, hands clasped on a large pocketbook. Smiling at me. It was hard for me to look at her and impossible to look away. All I could think was, She could be my mother. My mother and I might have played this scene. I'm twenty-nine years old and tomorrow she's sixty-five and we're meeting in an airport, a mother-daughter reunion at the gates, common as a cold.

I dropped my luggage and we embraced, and it took me a moment to let go of my mother's best friend, to raise my cheek from the soft cloth on her shoulder. When I did I noticed the lanky young man in a junior exec's suit at Dorothy's side—Jim, holding out his arms.

"C'mon, girl," he said. "Give me some sugar."

"Jimbo—you're a giant!" I was up on my toes to kiss his sunburned cheek. I stepped back and looked at Dorothy. "How tall is your bouncing baby boy?"

"Six-four," she said.

"And still growing," Jim said, patting his middle. He picked up my carry-on bag and portable typewriter.

"I'll get those," I said.

Jim made a face. "You're back in Tennessee now, Pamela. We don't let our women go trompin' around carryin' luggage."

"Okay boss," I said, linking my arm with Dorothy's, and we followed Jim through the airport and out to the car. Dorothy had a hitch in her step from hip surgery, and we talked about that, and Jim's job at a bank in town, and his wife, Lynn, and Jim's older brother Toby, who lived in Winston-Salem, where he was a dean at Wake Forest. Toby was thirteen years older than Jim, which had made him as unknowable to me when I'd visited with my mom as the interchangeable old ladies who'd welcomed my grandmother into their musty parlors.

Jim steered us along a highway that sloped through the hills, then onto a wide street of fast-food, auto-parts sprawl. We stopped at a Shoney's, and I sat with an overloaded salad-bar plate facing Dorothy and Jim. An older black man alone in the booth behind them opened a plastic bag and poured peanuts into his soda. I watched him gulp the salty sludge, jaws grinding as he swallowed. Now that I was in Kingsport all I wanted to do was talk about my mom. It had taken me fifteen years to get here and now I felt like I didn't have an hour to lose. I wanted to ask every question I could think of, hear everything about her that anyone could remember. I wanted other people's memories of her. Maybe they'd help me find some of my own. But I didn't want to spill my guts into my three-bean salad, so I watched the old guy drinking his strange brew and tried to be as gracious as my hosts, offering what I could in the way of small talk about Kevin and California.

As we climbed into the car again Jim said, "That was good. But I'll tell you what—there was no finer cuisine in Kingsport than the cheeseburgers and fries we ate by the pool at the Downtowner."

"At those wobbly tables," I said, catching his eye in the rearview mirror.

"Then jumpin' right back in."

"Attack of the human cannonballs."

"Oh *man*," Jim said, steering us back into traffic. "I'd be headin' out the door, Mom'd say, 'Where're ya goin'?' *'Goin' to the pool!'* "

Ten minutes down the road we rounded a turn and a mountain came into view.

"That's Bays Mountain," Dorothy said. "You remember goin' up Bays Mountain, don't you?"

"Sort of."

A few turns later a stack of windowless brick buildings filled the foreground at the base of the mountain, their tall chimneys chugging white smoke into a soot-colored sky.

"Is that the Eastman?" I asked, suddenly remembering the vernacular—always *the* Eastman.

"That's Mead," Jim said.

"What do they do?"

" 'At's a paper mill."

I lowered my window an inch. The air smelled like vinegar. Like rags soaked in vinegar.

"We're right proud of that smoke," Jim said, glancing in the rearview mirror. "That's that new improved *healthy* smoke we have in Kingsport now. Not like that bad old stuff we used to breathe."

"Oh *now*," Dorothy said, touching her son's sleeve. "Let's go up Broad Street and around the Circle. You remember Church Circle, don't you, Pamela?"

"Sort of."

Four nearly identical red-brick churches with white trim. Jim circled the landscaped roundabout, then headed down one spoke of the holy wheel. At the top of a steep incline, he turned left. This I remembered—the matching Tudor-style houses wrapped around a small park. I remembered sitting on the knotted roots of the old trees at the park's perimeter and walking up here from the Downtowner with my mom. In the dusty parlor of one of these Tudors, a friend of my grandmother's had offered a cut-glass plate of sandwiches made from canned date bread and cream cheese.

We pulled into Dorothy's carport and went through her side door into a wood-paneled kitchen. Jim carried my luggage upstairs and went home to his wife. Dorothy and I settled in her den.

"It's pretty amazing to be here," I said, looking around. Her armchair faced the TV. A tray table within reach held books and magazines. This would be where she spent most of her time now. The dark windows at my back looked onto the park. "I've been trying to remember the last time I was in Kingsport," I said. "I guess it would have been the summer before my mom died. Or maybe we didn't go to the Farm that year."

"You were here for your grandmother's funeral," Dorothy said.

"Oh. Right."

"You don't remember that?"

"Not really, no."

"You came up to me at the service and said, 'I'm so glad to see someone I know!' And then after, you all came over here."

Dorothy's hands seemed to be searching for something in her lap, her fingers like sightless creatures sensing their way on unfamiliar ground. "How's your father, Pamela?" she said, adjusting her glasses. "You haven't said a word about him."

"He's fine. He's good."

"He still in that big ol' house of yours?"

"Ah. I guess you've missed a few chapters."

"Well I knew he had some reversals. Business reversals."

"What a lovely Southern way to put it!" I said, laughing. "Yes, he reversed all the way to zero, basically. He went bankrupt."

"Well."

"Then he moved in with his girlfriend."

"I guess I heard somethin' about that."

"She's thirty years younger than him," I said, and we let that float in the lamplight between us. But I wasn't quite done. "She wears my mother's wedding bands, Dorothy. He gave her the rings my mother wore for twenty-two years. He had a teenage daughter at the time, but hey, no problem. He got those rings off my mother and stuck 'em on his girlfriend's finger."

"Oh law."

"Sorry," I said, as surprised as Dorothy at my outburst. I hadn't said a word to anyone about those rings in the decade my father's girlfriend had worn them. I didn't even know I was mad about the rings until now. "My father told me about Roy . . . passing," I said, trying to get back on track. "What year was that?"

"Roy died in 'seventy-four," Dorothy said. "See, it was just one year after Mildred."

"It was sudden, wasn't it? With Roy?"

"He just worked himself to death on that house," she said, and I knew what she meant. I remembered the story of Roy Hale building a cabin in the woods. He'd bought land and taken apart the structures on it, using the old wood to build his retirement home log by log.

"It was like he had two jobs," Dorothy said. "He'd go to the Eastman on the eight-to-three shift, then go on out there in the afternoon and work until dark. If he was on the night shift, he'd change clothes and work out there all day. He came home one day and went upstairs and lay down, and he never got up."

"I'm sorry."

"But see, now Pamela, I was out when the call came from Chicago, about your mother. When I came home Roy said, 'Mildred's dead.' And I didn't even know she was sick! I didn't know anything. I didn't know she'd had a mastectomy all those years before."

"Don't you think that's strange?" I asked, emotion gathering in my throat. "You were her best friend."

"Well I'm sure she had her reasons. I'm sure she was doin' what she thought was the right thing."

"Like not telling her teenage daughter that she had breast cancer."

"She was trying to protect you," Dorothy said, and a sob burst from me. Dorothy pushed herself up from her armchair and limped to the couch. She put her arms around me and we sat like that, rocking gently, her blind fingers tapping patterns on my back.

"People had different attitudes back then," she said when I'd calmed down. "You have to understand that it was a different time."

I wiped my eyes. "It's nice of you to make excuses for her."

"Don't be angry at your momma."

"They didn't tell me *anything,* Dorothy. Either of them. It was just poof! Your mom's gone."

Why couldn't I say "dead"? Roy *passed.* My mother was *gone.* I'd never had any trouble with *dead* before.

Dorothy sat back and looked at me. "Your life was good when you were younger," she said. "You all had so much. And don't you ever think your daddy didn't love your mother. When they got married he said to me, 'I didn't know people like this existed till I met Mildred.' "

I felt like a month had passed since I'd boarded the plane at LAX. I followed Dorothy's rocking gait as she climbed the narrow stairway to the second floor. At the top of the steps she entered a dark bedroom and flipped on a light. I stopped in the doorway and stared. Across the room, hanging between shuttered windows, was a large framed picture of a young boy. I walked toward it, magnetized. When I was close enough to touch the glass I saw that it had been made with pastels, loosely stroked, finger-smudged. A blue-eyed boy in a blue T-shirt. His smile had browns and pinks in the middle where front teeth were missing.

"Mildred gave that to me," Dorothy said. "After Tommy passed."

"How old was he?"

"Seven."

And I remembered the story—the middle son who died of leukemia. The son who'd come and gone in the thirteen years between Toby and Jim. Here he was in bright pastels, with neatly combed side-parted hair and a gap-tooth grin. It looked like my mother had worked from a school picture.

"Wow," I said, stupidly. All I could think was: Why didn't she ever make a picture of me?

Dorothy turned from the sink as I came in. A washing machine rumbled nearby. I went to the counter and laid my cheek on her shoulder and looked through the window at a bright patch of grass separating her mock Tudor from her neighbor's.

"I guess that's what you needed," she said, her hands busy with carrots and potatoes in the sink.

"I guess." Twelve dreamless hours. I poured a cup of coffee and took it to the table, where a fat scrapbook lay on a vinyl mat. "What's this?"

Dorothy turned off the tap. "I thought you might want to have a look in there," she said, limping over. She opened the scrapbook and held up a little pamphlet the color of a marigold.

"Do you know about this?" she asked. The pamphlet's gold cover showed a line-drawn woman in a hoop skirt, bonnet strings aflutter, standing by a picket fence. *Dixie Study Club, 1948–1949.*

"Never heard of it."

"Well your grandmother's in here," she said, "and your mother might be, too."

I took the pamphlet and skimmed typed quotes by Browning and Ben Franklin, a verse of "Dixie," pages of bylaws. The membership list was on the last page. "Mrs. H. R. Lady," my grandmother, was vice president that year.

I put the pamphlet down and paged through the scrapbook's newspaper clips, scanning the headlines.

DIXIE STUDY CLUB HEARS TALK ON FRANZ SCHUBERT

SOUTHERN NEWSPAPERS IS TOPIC OF DIXIE STUDY CLUB MEETING

DIXIE STUDY CLUB HONORS HUSBANDS, GUESTS AT CHRISTMAS
DINNER

The photos on the faded newsprint showed old-ladyish
middle-aged women in loose-fitting suits and flowing dresses,
wearing hats and gloves and bulky corsages, seated at tea tables,
standing by flags—soc-beat photos, circa 1940. I peered into the
stop-sign-shaped glasses on a round face that was fuller than I'd
ever known it. Mrs. H. R. Lady looked happy, in picture after
picture. Here in her world.

"Can I make copies of these?" I asked, but before Dorothy
could answer the screen door opened and a big man in rumpled
slacks lumbered in.

"Look what the cat dragged in!" he boomed.

"Hey there, Bruce," Dorothy said. "You remember my brother
Bruce, don't you, Pamela?"

I stood and held out my hand. "Hi Bruce."

Bruce Sullivan rocked back on his heels. "Mildred Lady's daughter," he said, his large palm swallowing mine. "From Chicago."

"Pamela lives in California now," Dorothy said.

"California!" he boomed, and strode from the kitchen, dropping onto the couch in the den with a heavy sigh.

Dorothy glanced at me from the sink. *Men,* her look said.
Brothers. What can you do?

"Can I get you anything, Bruce?" she called, but he didn't answer, and she went back to her work at the sink.

"You know that Southern writer," Bruce called after a minute.
"Wrote all about his family history? He wrote this book where
the main character's called Kunta Kinte."

"Alex Haley," I said, picking up my cup and joining him.

"This secretary over at the doctor's was reading that book the
other day," he said, looking toward the kitchen. "I asked her, 'You
know what Kunta Kinte means in English?' I said, 'It means
Leroy Jones!' "

Bruce and I listened to tapwater splashing into the sink. Then he looked at me. "How're ya likin' Tennessee?"

"It's gorgeous here," I said.

"What you journalists call 'a bucolic atmosphere.' "

"Hacks do, yes."

"How do you spell 'separate'?"

"There's a rat in the middle."

"A rat in the middle!" he boomed.

"I read that in a typing book."

Bruce was staring at the blank TV. His long legs reached halfway across the braided rug that filled the den.

"A learning-to-type book," I said. "Can I try another question? I'd like to go to the bonus round."

He didn't answer. I took a sip of coffee. I was in the armchair Dorothy had occupied last night until my wounded-animal sob brought her to the couch. Now I noticed the old photograph on the wall by the chair—a young bride in a simple white gown. The large print was blurry and brownish and looked like it was made early in the century. Dorothy's mother, I thought. Dorothy and Bruce's mother.

"Would you like some coffee, Bruce?" I asked, suddenly wanting to start over. I felt the tenuousness of my connection with these people, the lack of ties to my own. I was someone-they'd-once-known's grown-up kid, scratching at her roots.

Bruce didn't answer me. I took another sip from my cup. After a moment he said, "I remember your momma called me when I was in Nashville. 'This is Mildred Lady,' she said, and I went over there and saw her. She was real effervescent—I remember that. I only went over there the one time."

"Over where?"

His eyes flicked to me. "To the art school."

"What art school?"

"What was the name of that place, Dot?" Bruce called.

Dorothy came to the doorway, wiping her hands on her apron.

"I've been trying to think of the name of that school, but for the life of me I can't. We'll have to ask Vera Ruth tomorrow," she told me. "We'll see her at church. Vera Ruth and Grace Eller were into all that, art classes and drawin', and I think one of 'em might have applied to that school, too. But Mildred was the only one that went."

"To Nashville," I said.

"She was so excited about it," Dorothy said.

"My mother went to art school in Nashville."

"I saw her another time in Chicago," Bruce was saying. "She came down to the Palmer House—"

"Do you remember if it was a four-year school?" I interrupted.

Dorothy was studying me now. I'd seen this look last night. "I think it was," she said.

"Good." I got up. "Okay." I went upstairs for my shoulder bag, begging off breakfast, awkwardly shaking Bruce's hand again on my way out, promising Dorothy I'd be back soon, wouldn't get lost, had a map, don't worry, see you—

Every inch the ill-mannered Yankee. Back out in the vinegar air. Now I could slow things down.

How could I not know she went to art school?

How could she not tell me?

I walked to the Tudor four doors from Dorothy's, a duplex, 205 and 209 Compton Terrace. The street dipped in front of it, putting the duplex's dormer windows at eye level with Dorothy's carport. Dorothy had pointed out this house last night when I asked how she and my mother became such close friends—her family had lived in one half, she said, my mother's in the other. "The Taylor girls used to climb those trees," she'd said, pointing across the park, "and your mother and I would sit underneath playing with our dolls."

I turned from the duplex to the trees and tried to imagine the girls and dolls. My mother was born in 1923, so this would have been in the early years of the Depression.

Nothing. I needed a photograph. I needed study aids. I didn't even know what my mother had looked like as a little girl.

Using a map, I followed the hilly streets from Compton Terrace to Andrew Jackson Elementary School. Dorothy said it looked about the same as when they'd gone there. I was out of breath when I reached the hilltop schoolyard. I went to the swings at the edge of the property and sat down. From this angle I could see a stripe cut through the trees on Bays Mountain—a path to the radio antenna and three metal towers poking from its summit. The paper mill's chimneys and storage tanks jutted from the green carpet below. For the first time I noticed the white noise Mead produced along with its white smoke, a background thrum, like traffic on a distant highway. I sat on a swing and leaned back, pumping my legs until my feet reached into the pale sky. The swing's rusty chain creaked time.

Happy birthday to you
So you went to art school
Why didn't you tell me . . .
When you had a chance to?

"Henry was the shining light of the family," Dub was saying, glancing at the tape recorder balanced on his knee. I'd opened the Kingsport phone book when I got back to Dorothy's and found a dozen Ladys, among them "Lady, W. C., DDS"—my mother's cousin Dub. His office was on Stone Drive, a short walk from Dorothy's, and I found him alone there, finished with patients for the day but still wearing his lab coat. Dub was in his sixties, slim as ever, with dyed brown hair receded almost to his crown.

"Can I be proud of you for your mother?" he'd asked as we embraced. And that was all it took.

"Sorry," I'd said, digging in my bag for tissues. "Weird day."

"Come on back here and tell me about it," he'd said, and led me through the reception area to the cramped corner of an exam room, where we sat on folding chairs with our knees inches apart. I had my notebook out. Dub was fiddling with the tape recorder.

"Yessir," he said now, "your grandfather was quite a character."

"I never really heard about him," I said, my little outburst over. It would be a relief to talk about a grandfather I'd never known. Maybe I could get through this without any more blubbering.

"Henry was the oldest son, you know," he said.

"How many kids were there?"

"Let's see, there was Henry, then Lily, Mandy, Arch, Andrew, Burl and Willie, who died when he was in his teens."

"Lily was Lily Hite?"

"That's right."

"I was trying to figure that out—how Aunt Lily and Uncle Riley fit in. Why we stayed at their farm. So she was Henry's younger sister."

"That's right."

"And your dad was Arch?"

"That's right."

We talked a little about Arch and Andrew, who must have been my mother's favorite uncles, because we spent so much time with them when we were at the Farm. Arch wore skinny black ties and thick-rimmed glasses—he was the town mouse. Sunburned country-mouse Andrew had Black Angus cattle and royal-named dogs, Kings and Queenies and Dukes. Relaxing in a lawn chair, Andrew would tell his dogs to sing, and they'd point their long snouts up and howl.

"We used to go down to Henry's house when they were livin' over there by Dorothy's," Dub said. "I must have been seven or eight at the time. Your mother was a couple years ahead of me.

We'd play in that park. And 'course your grandfather was always sort of the center of things when you came to his house. Henry Lady could tell tales all night long. He had all the charm. He could tell the same thing over and over and it was still funny."

"I wish I'd known him."

"See, Henry had taken a little college work," Dub said. "I think it was a business school over in Jonesboro, so he had a greater education than most, and he could present himself. Most of the fellas had never finished high school, that he worked with."

"Where was that?"

"Well, first he had a job at Mead. Personnel manager, I think it was. He had a big job over there, and people that worked for him, they loved him, because he'd take care of them. He could manage people. Like I say, he was, he was, he hadda, he hadda lot goin' for him."

I was idly taking notes, as I would if I were interviewing this sweet-tempered Southern dentist for a newspaper story. Checked pants. Owlish glasses. Gray hair peeking out under the dye-dulled brown curls behind his ear. I stopped writing. Why the sudden stutter?

Dub recrossed his legs, shifting my tape recorder to his other knee. "The big problem was that Henry became an alcoholic. He belonged to the Masons, see, and the group he was with, I guess they got to partyin' and drinkin' and carryin' on. And he lost his job at Mead. This was in the late twenties, early thirties, 'round then. Then he got into selling *in*surance, and that didn't go too well either. He had two houses up there where Dorothy lives, and he lost them both. He bankrupt the whole family."

"He *bankrupt* the family?" I said, laughing. "Sorry—I know this isn't funny."

"It's good to see you laugh," Dub said, smiling. "Mildred had a beautiful laugh."

Oh, right. Her. I was just enjoying the irony, if that was the word: Daughter of a bankrupt, searching for her long-lost mother, discovers long-lost's dad was a bankrupt, too. A bad-fiction coincidence.

Dub told me Henry had forged his own father's name on a loan. "It wasn't a very big note," he said. "Three or four hundred dollars, seems like it was. But my granddad didn't have that money, and he lost his farm."

"Wow."

"And see, Dad signed some notes for Henry, and he had to take bankruptcy, too."

"Arch signed notes for Henry?"

"That's right."

"Did he lose his house? The house you grew up in?"

"We were able to save our house, because Dad had put it in my mother's name. And he paid off those notes, Dad did, after he took bankruptcy. We had five, six boarders most of the time. Mother was pretty bitter about all that."

"I bet."

"She tried to tell him. She'd say, 'I heard Henry's in trouble,' but Dad would say, 'Aw, there's nothin' to that—he's got two houses!' And Henry being the oldest son, and looked up to in the family, Dad was just mad as whiz at anybody who'd say, 'Your brother's a drunk. Your brother's runnin' around . . .' "

Dub's voice trailed off.

"Running around meaning having affairs?" I asked.

He pushed his glasses up on his brow and rubbed his eyes.

"It's okay," I said. "I'm just wondering about him, who he was. I never knew the guy."

With his glasses back in place, Dub looked at me with magnified eyes. "Nellie was quite a gal," he said. "I'm sure she knew about it, but she held her head up. Nellie held that family together."

"Okay."

"And 'course, once Henry got on up at the Eastman, he did

real well. But your grandmother, see, she worked at J. C. Penney's for years. All that time Henry had no job. And she had all kind of trouble with her legs, varicose veins in her legs, see, and she was a saleslady, standing all the time at her job."

"Where did they live after Henry lost the houses?"

"Nellie's mother bought a house down there by Dorothy's, where they lived on through until Henry died."

"When was that?"

"You know, I was thinkin' about that after you called," Dub said. "What year were you born?"

" 'Fifty-eight."

"Well, see, I remembered when your mother came down for Henry's funeral, she came down on the train, and she was real big, seven or eight months along."

T he next day was Sunday. We went to church.

As Dorothy backed her silver Honda from the carport I remembered her mentioning that she'd learned to drive after Roy died. Jim had pestered her into it, she said, and when she finally got her license she realized he was right—she didn't want to be dependent on her son, as she'd been on her husband, for every errand and appointment.

"Why didn't you learn to drive before?" I asked, as she turned onto Wanola Avenue.

She answered the question inside my question. "I don't know why Mildred and I never wanted to drive," she said. We were easing down Wanola's steep grade at walking speed. "It seems old-fashioned when you think about it now, especially with Mildred goin' off and havin' her big city life."

I wondered if this was how my mother would have driven if she'd outlived my father, a doubly cautious elderly novice. Dorothy made a left on Sullivan Street and guided us into the parking lot behind the First Baptist Church, on Church Circle.

I'd walked the same route yesterday after I left Dub, stopping at the address on Wanola he recalled as my grandparents' last— the house he said my great-grandmother White bought for her daughter Nellie and bankrupt son-in-law Henry Lady. It was only steps from Dorothy's, across the park from the duplex Dorothy and my mom had shared as kids, and I'd tried for the second time that day to conjure ghosts from tan mortar and brown trim. The Tudors of Compton Terrace and its feeder streets should have been full of ghosts for me, but I couldn't scare up a single one.

Pink magnolias I'd written, finally, and closed my notebook. I might as well have written *blue sky* or *green grass.*

The First Baptist Church of Kingsport was a brick box with a fenestrated cupola, giving it more the look of a civic building than a house of worship. Yesterday I'd stood on the parkway in front of it, dutifully sketching the compass positions of the Baptists, Presbyterians, Methodists and Episcopalians. Then I noticed that all four churches were topped with weathervanes instead of crosses. That made me laugh. A nod to the godlike power of weather, I'd thought. Weather was the farmer's cross to bear.

Broad Street led from Church Circle to a fortresslike train station several blocks south, the dead end of what would have been the main drag when my mother lived here. Now mall-drained. I didn't need to see the malls to know they were near. Walking along Broad yesterday I'd passed a Woolworth store, a Goodwill outlet, the paint-chipped Strand Theater, which had been converted to the Broad Street Used Furniture Mart. Farther along, the State Theater was a "Christian cinema," per a sign tacked to its marquee. Now showing THEY LIED TO US and SUPERCHRISTIAN.

A block off Broad I'd found the building I was looking for. I peered through the dusty plate glass beside the locked front door and saw, under ladders and construction debris, the long curved counter that had been the check-in desk. I climbed five flights on an outdoor staircase, passing scarred motel-room doors and the iron railings where we'd hung our swimsuits to dry. Around back I stopped and looked down. A low structure filled the courtyard. I stared at the gravel roof, trying to picture a watery blue rectangle, and wobbly iron tables, and the lounge chairs where my mom and Dorothy had spent hours chatting while their children took cannonball leaps into the Downtowner's pool.

Dorothy and I crossed the church parking lot now, and stepped inside. We took a stairway to the basement and soon I was standing in a small room filling with women Dorothy's age and older, my thoughts bouncing off the pale green walls as Dorothy introduced me to her friends.

"This is Mildred Lady's daughter . . ."

"This is Nellie Lady's granddaughter . . ."

I could barely make eye contact with the women smiling lipstick smiles at me, gently touching my shoulders and arms, telling me my momma was a wonderful woman, my momma was such a sweet person, *I remember your momma had a beautiful smile.*

Funny, I don't. Or not funny.

"Pamela, this is Marjorie Stair and this is Audrey Taylor," Dorothy said. "Remember I was tellin' you about the Taylor girls?"

"The tree climbers," I said.

"That's right," the taller Taylor sister said, giving me the first firm handshake of the day. She was slender, dressed in deep purple, with blond mixed into her short gray hair. "Dot and Mildred didn't get out and get dirty like Babe and I did," she said. "Dot played with Mildred more than we ever did 'cause they were awkward."

"We were tomboys," said her sister, whose direct gaze was the visual equivalent of her sibling's handshake.

"They couldn't climb those trees out in the park like we did."

"They were little ladies."

I was jotting the Taylor girls' phone numbers in my notebook when a woman in a red dress joined us.

"I'm Vera Ruth Rule," she said, pressing my arm. "I was just tickled when Dot told me you might be here today. There are so many special memories."

She produced an envelope from her patent-leather purse. "After Dot called I got to lookin' in my scrapbooks and I thought you might want these."

She slid a photograph from the envelope, a black-and-white of five young women leaning on a stone arch. Four of them in baggy white shorts and boxy tops—

"That's me there," she said, pointing. "Look at those skinny legs! I wish I had those legs now! And that's Grace, she's wantin' to meet you, too, and there's Ida and Edell and . . ."

—my mother. In a checked dress. With wavy shoulder-length hair.

"When was this taken?" I asked, my thick voice warning me I wouldn't get too many more words out.

"Summer of 'forty-one," Vera Ruth said. "This was a group of young people from the church. We went to church camp in Ridgecrest, North Carolina. I remember we didn't have an alarm clock and we wanted to go on that sunrise hike. Was that this time, Dot? Anyway . . ."

My head filled with wind-in-a-conch-shell sibilance. I was swimming out to my nineteen-year-old mother. She was taller than the others, and set off in her patterned dress like a model in a photo shoot. The others, in their solid-white separates, were background figures, even the one up front, sitting at my mother's feet. And there was that smile I was hearing about. You could see that it wasn't a reflex. When my teenage mother looked at the camera that day—that moment—she was happy.

Now the room was full of motherly and grandmotherly Southern women in pastels and bright jewel-toned clothes. I sat on a folding chair next to Dorothy, aware of how funereal I looked in my plain black dress. I'd thrown it into my bag at the last minute when I remembered about church, about going to church. In this church-basement classroom, as at an Orange County society party, my soc-beat uniform announced "I'm Not Like You." I just didn't feel so smug about it here.

I opened my notebook and copied the words attributed to John Wesley that had been neatly printed on the chalkboard: "Gain all you can. Save all you can. Give all you can." I couldn't make heads or tails of it. I was counting folding chairs and trying not to think how much I wanted a smoke when a stately woman with a tall puff of beige hair stepped to the front and used her hands to signal us, as you would small children, to be quiet. Pushing the sound down. It worked.

"Girls," she said, a honeyed drawl, "we have a guest today." She held out her palm to me. "This here is the daughter of Mildred Lady!"

Little murmurs filled the room. The teacher was waiting for me to say something. But the pressure gathering in my throat warned me not to try. I nodded at her, hoping she'd move on.

"Is your momma still with us?" she asked, her open hand still reaching out to me.

I looked down at my notebook. The blue lines blurred.

"Mildred passed some time ago," Dorothy said, answering for me.

"But she was our age!" the teacher said, as if there must be some mistake.

After the service I met Dub on the steps of the Presbyterian church.

"There she is," he said, opening his arms to me.

"Here I is." I felt a rush of warmth seeing him. Or maybe I was just glad to be outside again. We'd planned to visit my grandfather Henry's last surviving sibling, Amanda Lady. But first we had to stop at Dub's mother's house to deliver groceries.

"And I got her prescription," he said as we zipped down a sunny side street, away from the crowds on Church Circle. "She needs medicine for artificial tears."

"I could have helped her out this morning. I seem to have an endless supply of real ones."

"Is it gettin', is it gettin' to you?" A hard question for Dub.

"It is," I said, not wanting to make this kind man stutter again today, "but that's okay. Maybe that's why I'm here—so things can get to me."

Dub's eighty-two-year-old mom lived in a little house with a fresh coat of white paint on it and all the curtains drawn at noon. Small, frail, neatly dressed in slacks and a crepe blouse, Mary Lady was out in the yard watering her flowers as we pulled up. Her brown bob had a reddish tint in the sun, same as her son's hair, making me wonder if the widower and his widowed mother shared a hairdresser.

"Did you know Mildred Lady?" she asked, peering at me with her tiny dry blue eyes. Dub had gone inside with the groceries. He must have told his mother I would be with him today, and "Mildred Lady" was the part of whatever he'd said that she remembered.

"I did know her," I said. "A little bit."

"She was a good girl, Mildred was."

"That's what I hear."

"And her momma didn't never complain."

"Dub was tellin' me that."

"Nellie Lady never did have a short word," Mary said, giving her hose a shake.

When Dub returned, her arthritic hands clamped onto his lapels. He kissed her. "You look beautiful today, Momma," he said, and then we were off to Aunt Mandy's house.

Amanda Lady just outside town lived with her daughter Jean, who answered the door and led us to a parlor filled with dark furniture. The shades were drawn. A gilt-framed mirror hung above the couch where ninety-two-year-old Mandy sat, one hand draped over a cane. She wore a pale blue nightgown and a navy robe. White curls haloed her face. Her head shook slightly, Parkinson's vibrato it looked like, but her posture was erect.

Dub introduced me. Mandy nodded. She knew why I'd come, and she began as soon as I brought out my tape recorder.

"I've never seen many people as good as my daddy was," she said. "He was a religious man. He had a place at the barn that he'd go to pray every morning. He'd get down on his knees. He didn't care who heard him. I'd start to the barn to milk and turn back when I heard my daddy a-prayin'.

"Back then, there wadn't no money. And there wadn't no jobs. Daddy and Mother were hard-workin' country people, and they accumulated two farms at that time. The Simmons place had fifty-sixty acres in it, and the homeplace about the same. They grew tobacco, wheat, corn. Raised cattle. And they done for their children as best they could. Arch and Andrew went through high school up here in Fall Branch but they didn't get to go to college. Henry went to college at Johnson City and he was the only one that went. Jean was always sayin', 'Well, Momma, how come Uncle Henry went to college and you didn't learn to read?' I said, 'I didn't have time. I had to work.' I had to make a garden. I had cows to milk, chickens to take care of. I'd help hang tobacco and I'd help grade it and pack it on the truck. Ain't nothin' I haven't done on the farm except plow. I never did plow.

"You wanted to know about your granddaddy Henry, and I'm a-tellin' like it was. I don't remember just exactly when, but Henry got with the wrong crowd. I never did hear of Henry gettin' out and gettin' real drunk and doin' dirt like some. He just drank, and set off in the shade and talked. Get the liquor in him, why he'd just talk hisself to death. And that's when the trouble started."

I waited. Mandy gripped her cane. "What trouble was that?" I asked, and after a moment she spoke again.

"They'd moved to Kingsport, him and Nellie, and he was always dressed up nice, you'd think he was a millionaire. You never seen him in nothin' but a nice brown suit, flyin' around big.

"Henry come out here one mornin', when I was a-churnin', and he said, 'Kinch'—that was my husband, Kinchelow. He said, 'Kinch, let's go up to the barn and have a look at your hogs.' See, he didn't want me to know what he was a-goin' to do, but I knowed it anyway.

"They stayed up there a long time and when they come back

Henry said, 'Well, I'm a-goin' up the road.' And when he was gone I said to Kinch, 'You didn't let him have any money, did you?' Kinch said, 'I signed a note for him.' I said, 'You done stuck your name to that note, you just as well get ready to pay it. 'Cause he ain't got nothin' to pay it with.'

"See, Henry was runnin' around buyin' houses and gettin' other people to stick their names on the notes. He'd come up here when Daddy and Mother was old, and he'd put up the floweriest tales you ever heard. And they believed him. And he broke my daddy almost up. They signed notes for Henry and they lost the Simmons place. And the homeplace was put to court, and the last bid was put on it, everbody'd quit biddin', and then Kinch put a bid on it and 'course we took it. We paid dear for it, I'll tell you this.

"And Henry'd come by, dressed up fine as a fiddle, and he'd walk through the house a-talkin' and lookin' around, and Mother'd say, 'Well Henry, cain't you set down and stay with us a little while?' 'Oh, I've got to get back to town, I've got to do this and I've got to do that.' And that was the way it went. And they still thought he was perfect. Mother and Daddy both."

Dub and I stood by the creek behind his house and talked about his wife, who'd died of breast cancer a few years after my mother, and their son Brad, who'd died in a car crash when he was twenty-five. Brad was the only one of Dub's four kids I remembered at all, and only because I'd gone back to Evanston with a secret cousin-crush the summer I was nine or ten and he was fourteen or fifteen. At a picnic that summer Brad had sat on a table at dusk strumming a guitar and singing "King of the Road."

Dub told me about his other children, their jobs and marriages, his grandkids.

Then we went inside and he handed me a small unframed painting that might have gone for ten or fifteen dollars at the

Goodwill store on Broad Street. It was a picture of a dog standing in the marshy shallows of a river with a limp duck clamped in its jaws. Above the dog's head, the sky was pink-streaked ivory at the horizon, muddy blue on top. Any hobbyist might have painted that sky but there was something about the birddog's dead-eye gaze at the viewer—something focused and defiant— that I thought might separate this canvas from the rest of the Goodwill stock. Something anyone would see, not just the dead painter's daughter.

"Mildred made this for Arch," Dub said, "and it meant a whole lot to him. I want you to have it."

"Dub."

"Yes ma'am?"

"Do you have a jam jar?"

He took a step back, staring at me like that birddog.

"I think I've got some tears for your mom."

"C'mon now," he said, putting his hand on my back, "you need to be gettin' back to Dorothy's."

When we were in the driveway he handed me a set of keys. "I want you to take this car," he said. "I've got another one to get me around in. You'll need a car while you're here."

"I can't say no, right?"

"That's right."

So I said thank you, and stowed my treasure on the passenger seat. At the first red light I slipped off my shoes and pantyhose and tossed them in back.

I drove the routes I'd walked from Dorothy's—up to the school-yard, around Church Circle, down the swaybacked stretch of Broad Street from the quartet of weathervanes to the train station, where freight cars crawled past the clock tower but no passengers had disembarked since before I was born. The Mead paper mill was a few hundred yards off this end of Broad. Every now and then a one-beat blast from a train's horn broke through the huffing and chugging of the mill's pulping machines.

From the station I headed east to Wilcox Drive and followed Wilcox south to the squares on my Kingsport map that were blank except for the crisscross stitching of train tracks and words that sounded like a warning: INDUSTRIAL AREA. Traveling the blank map squares, I passed unmarked freight cars five abreast on parallel tracks. Gray silos, pod-shaped storage tanks and vast factories trussed with pipes filled the space between the pavement and the chimney-striped horizon. A soot-colored pile of what looked like crushed coal appeared at a bend in the road, as if a giant had emptied his ashtray near the guardrail. I passed a billboard framed with crewcut shrubs. THE TENNESSEE EASTMAN, I read as I drove. CHEMICALS, FIBERS, PLASTICS. I knew from books on local lore that Tennessee Eastman was a division of Eastman Kodak, and that other factories around here made cloth, glass, cement. Most of them had opened in the twenties, around the time my mother was born.

It wasn't until I stopped on the shoulder and unfolded my map that I noticed how the whale-body bulge of central Kingsport rode a seam of railroad tracks, with this industrial buffer zone separating the old part of town from its river. Kingsport floated on the Holston's south fork, a town with a river but not a river town, its vinegar air spiced with chemicals.

One day I drove to the county courthouse in Blountville, to look for records of Henry's alleged borrowings and land-grabs, and as I drove my head was full of Mandy's and Dub's remembrances. Dub said that in his last years Henry "looked kinda like W. C. Fields." That made me smile. Mandy said her brother "got on the wrong road for a long, long time, but I didn't hold it against him, though I knowed he done wrong." I wanted to believe her. All I'd known of Henry Lady before this trip was his name. That blank was now amply filled by a smooth-talkin' moonshine-guzzlin' family-swindlin' grampa. I found it hard to be mad at him.

Fishing in my shoulder bag as I drove, I removed a photocopy I'd made at the library on my way out of town. Henry's obituary in the *Kingsport Times-News*. I'd only had to buzz through a couple rolls of microfiche to locate the announcement. Henry had died on June 15, 1958. Which meant my mother *was* hugely pregnant at her father's funeral, as Dub had recalled. Pregnant with me. Could I hang my fond feelings for my unknown granddad on that tenuous cord?

I parked across the street from the courthouse and walked to a bell the size of a medicine ball mounted on pillars near the entrance. The bell had hung atop the old courthouse for a century, according to the plaque nearby. In 1979, commemorating Sullivan County's two hundred years on the map, the bell was brought down and put on display by the door. I felt like a kid on a field trip as I made my way inside, following signs to the room on the second floor where the county's deed books were stored, open to the public. The walls were lined with thin shelves, each supporting one oversize volume. Several men in suits were working at tables in the center of the room. I was scanning the dates filigreed on the books' red leather spines when a fortyish lawyerish type with thick hair stiff as meringue blustered in. The others took note.

"Here's trouble," one said, chuckling.

"Thought you'd be on the back nine by now," said another.

The newcomer pushed the last of a candy bar into his mouth and shot the crumpled wrapper into the trash. "Hey y'all," he said, chewing. He hoisted his briefcase onto a table, popped open the buckles. "You see the paper this mornin'?" he said. "You know what the four scariest words are right now, fellas? *'I is your president!'* "

Right. I'd read the wire-service story in the local rags, too. Jesse Jackson made a stump speech yesterday. You didn't need to take a poll to see that these were George Herbert Walker Bush men.

I pulled one of the big books from its shelf and carried it to an empty table, bracing its metal-bracketed spine against my shoulder bag. With fresh notepad and new felt-tips, I got to work.

The first document I found with Henry Lady's name on it was dated June 1930. Ten months earlier, in August 1929, he'd borrowed "$102, secured by a Trust Deed on certain household chattels." Now, "said indebtedness has been paid in full." Between loan date and its payoff, the stock market had crashed, sending bankers and their cartoon likenesses leaping from window ledges. But Henry had gotten his furniture out of hock. Nice work, Gramps.

I found more of the same later that month, as Henry and Nellie were jointly released from loans on their Compton Terrace home. A debt of $1,370, borrowed from "L. P. Dashiell and wife, Louise G.," in 1928 was "paid in full." I checked the obit. Henry was thirty-six in 1928, when he'd signed the note. The thirty-six-year-old father of my five-year-old mom. Dub had given me a photo of her at about five, the earliest one I'd ever seen. She was wearing a dress with rickrack trim and she had a pageboy haircut—the same one she'd given me at that age. I wondered if she'd cried as I did when her silky curls fell to the floor. And I wondered how much Henry's $1,370 debt translated into in 1988 dollars. If this were a newspaper story, I would want to get that stat.

But this wasn't journalism, it was something else entirely, and I could feel its otherness weighing on me as my notebook pages filled. No sooner had Henry paid off the Dashiells than he offered his home as collateral to a local bank for $2,250, payable in "28 semi-annual installments" of seventy dollars, plus 6 percent interest. According to the payment schedule, the house on Compton Terrace would be debt-free again in September 1945.

Henry borrowed from banks and finance companies and people who must have been his friends. He bought one property at an auction held "at the front door of the Court House in Blountville" half a century before I passed through the same door to read all about it in a leather-bound deed book.

One year he needed three hundred dollars badly enough to offer up the entire contents of his home. An "Oak Ice Box" was put up as collateral, and a "Rockwood Range." Kitchen table and dining room set and an "Overstuffed Living Room Suite." Three beds were listed, rockers, wardrobes, bookcases, desks, rugs, "and all other goods both useful and ornamental, including dishes, silverware, cooking utensils, linens, pictures and all other household appurtenances not listed above."

An "Ellington Piano, No. 61278."

A "Minnesota Sewing Machine, No. 4168."

I left the book splayed on the table with my notes and went out to sit by the historic bell. I was thinking about my grandmother's Singer sewing machine, in the corner of her pink kitchen in Evanston—in "Nellie's Diner." The Singer was built into a table with wooden wings that unfolded to reveal a heavy black sewing machine hanging on a hinged base. I used to fish out the Singer for my grandmother after she grew too weak to do it herself. I threaded needles for her when her eyes weakened, and loaded bobbins into the little housing where the needle struck.

My grandmother had tried to teach me how to sew but I was impatient, inept. "Goodnight *nurse!*" she'd mumble, watching my erratic pressure on the foot pedal and tug-of-war with fabric.

My mom sewed, too, but she didn't use patterns. My mom bought huge swaths of cloth at Vogue Fabrics on Main Street, and stood at her turquoise closet holding the material against her body, studying herself in the full-length mirror by her turquoise dresser. She made a velvet dress with bright flowers blooming on a black background that she wore when she went out with my dad. She made a brown wool cape and wore it everywhere that year, even to church.

Henry and Nellie Lady were parties to five legal filings in 1931 alone, and four more the next year. Their shifting fortunes were detailed in twenty-eight documents dating from 1926, when my mother was three years old. One of the earliest deeds was handwritten in an ornamental cursive that filled two pages with capital letters as intricate as clef symbols, and lowercase *y*'s and *g*'s curling like ribbons on a gift.

Nellie's mother Eliza White had bought a house on West Wanola Avenue in 1942, passing it on to her daughter and bankrupt son-in-law when she died two years later. So Dub had gotten that detail right, too.

In the last document I found, dated 1965, the Wanola Avenue house passed from my widowed grandmother to a couple named Neeley for five hundred dollars "cash in hand" and a mortgage "payable in annual installments falling due March 15." The Ides of March. Goodnight nurse. I put down my pen and rubbed my eyes. My grandmother would have been due a mortgage payment on March 15, 1973, the day she buried her daughter—

It was time to go. I shelved the deed book and stashed my notes. It wasn't until I was back on the highway, wind splashing my hair around, that I remembered I'd booked an interview, and I was late.

First thing is, you look like your mother," Virgie Cox said, standing at her door.

Virginia and John Cox lived in a little frame house with green shutters on Sevier Avenue, three blocks from Compton Terrace. Dorothy had suggested I call the Coxes, who'd known my grandparents before my mom was born.

I was apologizing for being late when Virgie took my hand and led me to the sofa in the front room. Small and slender and limber as a gymnast, Virgie settled in an overstuffed chair with one thin leg drawn up so that the bare heel of her foot almost touched her bottom. Her tinted glasses and fan of white hair gave her a modish look, like Laurie Anderson in her ninth decade.

"Don't you think she looks like Mildred?" Virgie asked her husband.

John Cox sat beside me on the couch. "Mmm-hmm," he hummed. "She does, Shug."

"I see 'at more'n I see Missus Lady."

"Mmm-hmm."

I brought out my tape recorder. "Anything about Henry or Nellie or my mom," I said, "I'd love to hear it."

Virgie nodded. "Well, when we come up here from Knoxville, we got an apartment with Henry and Missus Lady."

"The brick house," John said. "We had the upstairs. Remember, Shug?"

"I do, but then when I's pregnant, Missus Lady give me room downstairs, didn't she, Daddy? And she wanted to keep us, but Henry said, 'Well, you don't want a couple that's got children.'

And Missus Lady said, 'Well, Henry, they're gonna get 'em here anyway, so just might's well!'"

Virgie and John—Sugar and Daddy—looked at each other and laughed.

"Your granddaddy could sell buttermilk to a cat," Virgie said, turning to me. "He'd just work you to death. We had a porch swing on that house, and when I's pregnant, and it was 'bout time for John to come from the plant, I'd go out there and sit in the swing. Well, here'd come Henry and he'd set down and start tellin' me 'bout the war—same thing every time. I could tell you 'bout the war good as Henry."

"Tales of his bravery in battle?" I said.

Virgie snorted. "Yeah, that's Henry all over."

"We got a book we're gonna let you take back," John said, clearing his throat.

"I told Daddy, I said, 'I wouldn't know anybody that I'd rather give it to.' On account of Mildred," Virgie said.

"And Miz Lady."

"Missus Lady was one of the most wonderful women that I have ever known," Virgie said. "And when you live together in a house like we did, we just almost was like a family together. That's where Son was born."

"Mmm-hmm."

" 'Fore Son come along, I'd keep Mildred, so Missus Lady could go to her meetings at church."

"Was she a good baby?" I asked.

"Oh, good! She was *perfect*," Virgie said. " 'Cept, see, she didn't want to go home! 'Cause Missus Lady wouldn't give her anything but zwieback, and I kept vanilla wafers! So I'd give Mildred vanilla wafers and that would just please her to death."

John had gone up the stairs by the front door and now he returned with a red candy box. Virgie sat up straight as he handed it to her.

"This here is Son's curls," she said, opening the heart-shaped box. "He wouldn't go to school till I cut his curls." We looked at the auburn tail tied with blue ribbon. Then Virgie leaned so close I could see her eyes studying me behind her tinted glasses. "You can't replace family, can you?"

"No, um, I guess you can't," I said, looking away. I asked John about working at the paper mill with Henry. A few minutes later I heard myself saying, "One of my cousins was tellin' me that Henry got to drinkin' around that time." As if drawling was contagious. Maybe it was. Yesterday, talking with Dorothy, I'd mentioned "this fella I used to date." Though not that the fella was a coke deala.

"Henry didn't drink on the job, Daddy," Virgie said suddenly, as if contradicting something John had said.

"Well I know, Shug," John said, "but later on, he *did* drink. He did drink some."

I asked if drinking was the reason Henry got fired.

Virgie shook her head. "It was on account of that colored woman, wadn't it, Daddy?"

"Well, yeah."

"When he hit that colored woman—that was the start of Henry gettin' his walkin' papers," Virgie said.

I asked what had happened.

"Well, he was goin' up Center," John said, "and then it was somewhere about Sevier Avenue, where Sevier crossed Center."

"That was where the coloreds lived back then," Virgie said.

"Mmm-hmm. Somewhere 'tween there and just above it, was where it was."

"Henry was driving?" I asked.

"Henry always had a big Ford car, with the isinglass windows," Virgie said.

"So he hit a woman while he was driving? We're talking about an accident?"

"That's right," Virgie said.

"Did he kill her?"

"I believe he did," Virgie said.

"I don't know whether she died then or she died later," John said. "She died."

"He got out of it, but he lost his job right after that," Virgie said.

"How did he get out of it?"

"Well, he got a good lawyer, I guess," John said.

"They made a settlement," Virgie said.

"Mmm-hmm. I think there was some kind of a settlement."

I have my mother's high school yearbook," I said into the phone.

"Hoo-ee," Kevin said. "How'd you manage that?"

"Not *hers*. But she's in here." And then I was crying, as I knew I would when I came down to the kitchen from Dorothy's guest room for my nightly call. I'd brought the yearbook with me, a *1941 Maroon and Grey*—the book Virgie and John Cox had wanted to give Mildred Lady's daughter. I blew my nose and didn't try to talk for a minute or two. Kevin knew he didn't have to fill the line. We'd had some practice at this.

The Coxes' son, whose first curls were preserved in a Valentine's candy box, had been in my mother's class at Kingsport's Dobyns-Bennett High School, where he'd worked on the yearbook staff. The book Virgie and John had given me had their names on the inside flap and edit marks throughout. Among the spelling corrections in this copy from what must have been the penultimate print run were little notes of encouragement to the yearbook staff. "Good!" scribbled by a caption. "Nice shot!" slanting near a photo.

"I wish I could be with you," Kevin said.

I turned to the senior portraits. " 'Mildred Lady,' " I read aloud. " 'Band 1, 2, 3, 4; Debate Club 1, 2, 3, 4; Art Club 3; Journal Club 4. National Honor Society.' "

"Impressive."

"She was pretty amazing-looking," I said, my voice disappearing.

"This is tough," Kevin said.

"Dorothy says my eyebrows are like hers," I whispered, and we had to wait again. When I could talk I said, "Things are just kind of coming to me here."

"I can't wait to see."

"People are giving me amazing things."

"This is hard work."

"I don't know what it is," I said. "I go to people's houses and turn on my tape, and pretty soon I'm blubbering away. Then the people I'm in-theory interviewing babysit me until I get it back together."

"You're doing great."

I closed the yearbook. "What's happening there?"

"Not much. Work. You got something from Allan."

"What do you mean?"

Kevin lit a match. I heard smoke and breath shush past the receiver. "It's not important," he said. "Forget it."

"Forget *what*? Did you open it?"

"No, but I know what it is."

"So what is it?"

"You don't need to be thinking about Allan right now."

"I'm thinking about him now that you mentioned him."

"Look," Kevin said, "with his usual sense of timing, Allan has decided that this is the time to tell the story of his life."

"Is this about those columns?" I said. "I know about the columns." My father had been writing personal essays for a suburban giveaway paper. He sent me his clips. I stuffed them in a file unread.

"He thinks he's going to write a book," Kevin said.

"About what?"

"His life."

"So he wrote to say he's writing a book?"

"He sent a chapter."

"Did you read it?"

"He called," Kevin said, exhaling heavily. "He told me about it. I don't want to read it."

The *1941 Maroon and Grey* lay in a custard-colored cone of light. I switched off the wall lamp and sat in darkness at Dorothy's kitchen table, tracing the raised letters on the yearbook's cover.

"You're right," I said, finally. "I don't want to think about Allan."

Marjorie Stair and Audrey Taylor, the tree-climbing Taylor girls I'd met in the church basement, stopped by the next morning. I was drinking coffee and reading the *Kingsport Times-News*.

"Avon calling," Audrey said, coming through the screen door. She was in purple again, her bright sweater reminding me of the dress she'd worn to church. "Well look here." She went straight to the Dobyns-Bennett yearbook I'd left on the table last night. "Where'd you find this old thing?"

"Do you know the Coxes?" Dorothy said. "Up on Sevier?"

"That's not King's folks, is it?"

"No. John Cox Jr.'s their son."

"That's right," Audrey said, paging through the yearbook. She slowed as she reached the senior portraits. Then she held the book up and looked from it to me. "You look like your momma from here up," she said, leveling a salute on the bridge of her nose.

"King Cox sang at your momma's wedding," said Marjorie, the shorter, darker Taylor sister. She wore large round glasses and spoke with precise diction. As she looked at me I felt like I was being watched by a super-intelligent bug. "King Cox sang in a lot of weddings back then."

"I'd forgotten that," Dorothy said, taking a pitcher of tea from the fridge. "King had a real nice voice, didn't he?"

Audrey snapped the yearbook shut. "Well go on, Babe. What're you waitin' for?"

Marjorie was holding a grocery bag behind her legs, and now she brought it around and handed it to me. "I've had these in my attic since I don't know when," she said. "I can't say exactly how they got there, but I figure I must'a had 'em all these years so I could give them to you."

Inside the bag were two small unframed paintings, murky with grime.

"She made 'em when we was kids," Marjorie said.

Gently, I pulled them out. One was a picture of a barefoot boy in a wide-brimmed hat, whistling as he walked a forest path downhill. The other showed a shirtless Indian brave in feathered headdress watching from a rocky outcropping as a wagon train threaded the valley below.

Mildred E. Lady—a brushstroked signature.

I had to fight the urge to run upstairs with the canvases. All of a sudden I wanted to be alone. But I had to do this first, so I followed along as Dorothy led us through the den and into the living room.

"I guess you told her about how we used to get together and make chocolate candy," Audrey said to Dorothy. She pulled an armchair close to the couch, where Marjorie and I had landed. Dorothy settled in a chair by the windows. "That was the silliest thing," Audrey told me. "We'd get together, the four of us, and one'd furnish a cup of sugar, another'd bring the butter. None of us had the ingredients for the full recipe."

"You just stirred it in a skillet," Marjorie said.

"Or they'd come to our house and we'd make chocolate cake with seven-minute frosting."

"I remember that," Dorothy said.

"We never really played a whole lot in Mildred's house," Marjorie said, " 'cause her mother didn't like the house messed up."

"If we were over there, we stayed in the basement, more or less," Audrey said.

"Or we were out in the park," Marjorie said.

"See, we didn't have any classes together," Audrey said. "Us'n Mildred. Our only association was playing together, and church."

Dorothy nodded. "We used to do our studyin' when the women were in church meetings. And we went into that little living room and did our homework, and I always wondered what was going on through those doors over there."

"Did you all ever go over to those scary movies with us when they'd have Eastern Star meetings?" Audrey asked. "Over at the Strand Theater?" *Thee-ate-er.*

"And after the meetings we used to go in and sit in those big chairs," Marjorie said.

"Leather chairs," her sister said.

"We thought that was the greatest thing . . ."

My attention drifted as the friends reminisced. I'd leaned my mother's paintings against the couch by my legs—I didn't want to let them out of my reach—and now I picked them up.

Audrey turned to me. "Your momma had an interest in drawing even when she was in grade school," she said. "And I did, too. I used to sit on the porch and draw for hours and hours. And when your momma got to high school and she still had that interest in drawing, they had the money to send her to art school. Well, we didn't have the money, so mine just went *ka-blew.*"

"Before she married," Marjorie said, "your momma come home and she had these pretty gowns. You remember those gowns, girls? Oh! They was pleated, accordion pleats, all the way down, in pastel colors. I'd never seen a gown like that. How many colors did she have?"

"Five, I think it was," Dorothy said.

"She said she paid thirty dollars apiece!" Marjorie said. "And I'll tell you what, thirty dollars back then was a month's salary."

"I remember them gowns," Audrey said.

Marjorie's round lenses caught the light from the window. Bug-eyed, she smiled at me. "We just thought that was the cleverest thing."

I asked the sisters if they'd kept in touch with my mother through the years.

"One time we went up to Chicago," Marjorie said. "We called in on your momma, and your daddy took us around. We went over to Northwestern University. 'Course he had that big Cadillac, and I'll tell you, if that didn't impress my boys!"

"We always got together in the summers," Audrey said. "You all'd stay down at the Downtowner and you'd come to this park about every day."

"I remember this one time," Marjorie said. "It was Mildred and Dot and Audrey and myself, and all the children playing in the park. And your mother was telling—and she was very modest about it—but she said Northwestern University had a program for gifted children, and I forget what percentage but only the very top percentage got to go. And it was most unusual for two children in one family to be selected to attend this program. And both you and your brother had been selected, but your momma didn't want to saddle you with school year-round. She said she preferred you spending your summers in the mountains and parks of Tennessee. I remember her saying that. So you'd know where your people come from."

When the Taylor sisters left I took the paintings upstairs and stood them on the dresser, next to the canvas Dub had given me. Birddog, meet Tom Sawyer and Indian Brave. I sat on the bed and stared at them.

Judging by palette and skill level, they'd been made around the same time. *When we was kids.* I glanced at the pastel of Tommy, a mature effort of my mom's, dating from a few years before I was born. Transcribing my tapes in the evenings I turned my back on Tommy. I couldn't deal with Tommy. But I'd keep my new triptych where I could see it as I worked.

The Taylors had suggested that I call another friend of my mother's, Grace Eller, to find out more about the paintings. I'd met Grace at church, too, and when I called she told me again that my mother was "a very pretty girl" with "a lot of confidence." I drummed on my notebook, impatient with her kind words. Like Vera Ruth Rule, who'd given me the photo of my teenage mom and her four friends at church camp, Grace now recalled that my mother had registered at Carson-Newman, a Baptist college near Kingsport, and changed her plans at the last minute to go to Nashville. But Grace couldn't remember the name of the art school either.

We were saying goodbye—my notebook page blank—when Grace mentioned another classmate from Dobyns-Bennett. "Maryana Smith knows about that art school," she said. "She lives over in Johnson City now."

"Maryana Smith," I repeated, taking notes.

"Smith *Huff,* now," Grace said. "Oh, and one other thing I was just rememberin'. Your mother liked to wear scarves. She liked to put little touches of color to her outfits that way. Did she still do that when she was grown up?"

She did.

She had dozens of silk scarves.

What happened to her scarves?

Maryana Smith's senior portrait was one page away from Mildred Lady's in the *1941 Maroon and Grey*—a soft-featured smiling girl with loose curls framing an oval face. She looked like a go-along get-along kind of girl, and the sixty-five-year-old Maryana Smith Huff I met at her mother's house in Johnson City seemed that way, too. Like the others who'd known my mother as a schoolgirl, she wasn't surprised that I'd come to see her with my tape recorder and questions. What I hadn't been able to put into words before I left California—what was I doing, exactly? what was I looking for?—was wordlessly understood. A daughter wants to know about her mother. Simple as that.

At lunch, Maryana's mother was the best-dressed of the three of us. Margaret Lyons Smith, who must have been about ninety, came out slowly from a back room wearing a white-striped jersey dress, stockings and low-heeled shoes. Before we tucked into plates of ham and greens, she handed me a copy of her recently published first novel, a Civil War story titled *Miss Nan, Beloved Rebel.* At the end of the meal, she wrote "Thank you Pamela" on the title page above her wavy autograph. Then I watched the small, plump white-haired daughter take her smaller, slender white-haired mother's hand and lead her slowly back to her bedroom for a nap.

I waited, sitting on another floral-print couch, surrounded by another collection of family mementoes. I realized that I'd never put a photo of my mother in any home I'd made for myself in the decade since my father moved in with his girlfriend. I knew I had a few, in a box somewhere. I tried to recall a picture of her on display in Evanston, and couldn't.

When Maryana returned, she began with my mother's laugh. "Mildred just laughed all over," she said. "When things tickled her, I can just see her now, shakin' her shoulders. Did she still do that?"

"I don't know," I said. "I don't really remember her laugh."

"Well, Mildred was so much fun," Maryana said, keeping things rolling. "And she had such a brilliant mind."

"That's nice of you to say."

"But it's true! She knew all about politics because her dad loved to talk about politics, and they talked about it at the table at night. That's one of the reasons the boys liked Mildred so much! She knew all about politics and all about ball, because she went to all the ballgames with the band."

Band 1, 2, 3, 4. "Do you remember what instrument she played?"

"Mildred played the piccolo," Maryana said, and described my mother in her band uniform, slim and athletic-looking, with shiny hair and the touches of color at her neck that Grace Eller had recalled. "Now let me tell you about the boyfriend."

"Please do."

His name was Elliott Armbrister, and he worked in the cafeteria at the Eastman. According to Maryana, she and Elliott had been dating for a year the night he met my mom at a party on Bays Mountain. Soon, Elliott was Mildred Lady's boyfriend.

"I was kind of miffed at her for taking my boyfriend," Maryana said, laughing, "but then I found out nobody really knew I was datin' him! And I did talk to him a little bit about datin' her, and you know, he was just crazy about her, so I decided I wouldn't be mad."

When we got around to the paintings Dub and the Taylor sisters had given me, Maryana listened to my descriptions, nodding.

"She made those at Miz Hurt's," she said. "Mildred and I took art classes from Miz Hurt when we were in junior high. She had a big old chest of drawers where she had pictures you could choose from, and she taught us how to enlarge by measuring and all of that. Her husband made the frames for us, and stretched the canvas, and we painted at her dining room table. She was excellent at what she taught us, but later, when your mother got to art school, she was a little bit sorry that we had learned that particular method."

"Do you remember the name of the art school?"

"Well I sure do—I was right there when the whole thing started! We were looking in the newspaper for something to draw, and we saw an ad for an art school in Nashville. So we decided to try this picture they said to draw, and we both mailed in our drawings and their recruiter came to see us! He told us this was a commercial school, and they would help you find a job after you graduated. And your mother decided right then and there that she was going, and that was that.

"And when we both got home from college after our first term your mother came to see me and she told me she was learnin' a whole lot. One thing she told me was make a file of pictures. She said, 'Miz Hurt was right about that.' She said, 'If you want to draw a horse and you don't know what one looks like, you can draw from a picture of one.' And then she told me some other things I debated whether to tell you or not."

"Things you think I don't want to hear?"

Maryana looked down the hall, toward the room where her mother slept.

"I'm just trying to get an idea of what my mom was like," I said. "Anything you can tell me, I'd be grateful to hear."

"Well, I was real glad I hadn't gone with her to that school," she said, turning to me, and then she laughed. "Because I would have turned around and come home! She said they had nude models for their drawing, and I asked her where you *looked.* She said, 'Well, Maryana, you look at everything, and you just draw the best you can.'

"And then she told me that the girls in the dorms didn't wear any clothes to sleep in! Like you hear about a nudist colony? I just couldn't have taken that."

That reminded Maryana of another thing she didn't know if she could tell me.

"I'm interested in everything about her," I said.

"Well, when we went to bed that night, see, she slept in the nude. And her mother came in, and I had on my pajamas, and Miz Lady said, 'Mildred! Put some clothes on!' First Miz Lady just whispered, you know. Finally she just opened the door and she came in there and she said, 'Well, put your panties on anyway! I'm ashamed for Maryana to know that my daughter sleeps in the nude.'

"And then I heard Mildred and her mother whispering outside the door, and Mildred said, 'Well, Mother, I'm not goin' to put my panties on.' Just matter-of-factly—not sassy or anything. She just didn't let anybody bother her, not even her own mother."

Later, after I'd packed away my copy of *Miss Nan, Beloved Rebel,* Maryana showed me around her garden. As I was getting back into Dub's car, she remembered one more thing to tell me.

"When Mildred came back to Kingsport after her first year, she had to make money to go back to school," Maryana said. "So she and I went over on the bus to Johnson City, and we went to the John Sevier Hotel, where there was a USO. And she set up her easel and her pad and charcoals and she sat right down and drew those boys. Drew 'em fast as she could make 'em, and sold those drawings for ten, fifteen dollars. She sorta charged according to how good she thought it was. And that was a lot of money! But those boys came to her one right after the other, and took her pictures away.

"And I never would try," Maryana said. "Your mother said to me, 'You never will learn if you don't try.' But I didn't have the confidence your mother had. She just did her own thing. She was very free."

The Nashville operator came up empty. I asked if she'd check listings outside the city. Maybe "Nashville" meant *near* Nashville to my mother's friends, the way "Chicago" was my shorthand for Evanston.

"I've got a 'Harris School of Art' in Franklin, ma'am."

"Bless you," I said, for the first time in my life, and poked the numbers into Dorothy's kitchen phone. I wasn't quite ready for the voice that interrupted the second ring.

"Hi," I said, clearing my throat. "I'm calling for—I guess some general information. I was wondering if someone there had a moment—"

"I'm Beth Harris. What can I help you with?"

"Mrs. Harris—hi. I'm calling to try to find out if your school is the one my mother went to. She would have been a student there about fifty years ago. I don't know if your records—"

"What's your mother's name?"

"Her name was Mildred Lady," I said. "I'm Mildred Lady's daughter." Two weeks ago, in a church basement, those words stung my eyes like flung sand. Now they were mine.

"Mildred Lady's daughter," the voice in the phone repeated. "Your daddy the one she worked for in Chicago?"

"That's the one."

"Can't recall his name."

"Allan Marin."

"The daughter of Mildred Lady from Kingsport and Allan Marin from Chicago. Let's see, you'd be about thirty-five years old."

"Twenty-nine," I said. "My mother was kind of an older mom for her generation. Mrs. Harris, I was wondering—"

"Beth."

"Beth. I was wondering if I could come talk to you. I'm in Kingsport right now, visiting some of my mother's friends."

"Your mother passed?"

"Yes."

"How long ago?"

"Fifteen years ago. She died when I was fourteen."

The line was quiet for a moment. "Have you got a car over there in Kingsport?" Beth Harris asked.

I jotted her address and the directions she gave me in my Week-At-a-Glance. When we hung up I looked at the names and addresses filling dates in March and now spilling into April: My mother's Life-At-a-Glance. Then I opened Dorothy's phone book. I'd drive to Nashville tomorrow. That left time for the boyfriend today.

Elliott Armbrister was standing in front of his brick house a couple miles east of Dorothy's as I pulled up in Dub's car. Since he was home midmorning midweek, I figured he was retired. Which meant he'd dressed for our talk, I thought as I cut the engine, noting the red tie pinned in place on a white shirt, razor-creased gray slacks, black dress shoes. He was tall and powerfully built. I got out and shook his hand.

"Let me just start by saying you look like your mother," he said. "Oh, yes."

"Thanks—I mean, thanks for letting me come by today."

"She was slender like you," he continued, squinting in the brightness, "and she wore her hair a little longer than yours. And she was a little taller."

I'm taller, I thought, as we stepped inside, but that's sweet. She's grown in his memory.

Elliott's wife was laying out cookies and lemonade on a side table in her pin-neat living room. Also dressed up for our chat, in nylons and a belted dress on this muggy spring morning.

"I'm Irene," she said, turning. That's when I saw the silver canister of oxygen at her feet. "We're so glad to meet you." The clear plastic tube tethering her to the canned air bounced with the motion of her mouth.

We started with their children—everyone I was meeting seemed to enjoy that subject—and threaded our way back through Elliott's recent retirement from the Eastman to his first lunchroom job there in the late thirties. He'd come to Kingsport from Virginia, he said, and recalled some of the same picnics and parties Maryana had told me about, though he didn't mention her.

"Mildred always talked about wantin' to be a commercial artist," he said. "I remember I gave her a book of famous paintings, a big brown book. I guess it was Christmas of 'thirty-eight. She had an uncle who was wantin' her to paint a picture of a huntin' dog."

Birddog. Mine now.

"And I remember, I believe it was Valentine's Day, I took her to the movies and we stopped at the drugstore and got a soda. And I bought her a box of Whitman chocolate candies. And it embarrassed the dickens out of her! She just didn't want me to spend money on her."

Irene Armbrister had been sitting quietly, her oxygen tank like a basset hound at her ankles, the slack tubing curled in her lap. Now she piped up. "Don't forget to tell her about—Mildred didn't kiss anybody."

"Oh, well, now," Elliott said softly, his large hands knitting together in his lap.

That evening, as I transcribed my tape, I was surprised to hear the hiss of a match and hard intake of breath when I got to that part of the interview. I'd lit a cigarette! Mrs. Armbrister was sucking canned air—and I'd lit up.

"Did Mildred smoke?" Elliott asked on the tape. I pressed *stop*. I could hear the floorboards creak in Dorothy's room across the hall. Maryana had asked me the same question yesterday, and when I'd laughed and said I couldn't imagine my mother smoking, Maryana's gentle response hit a chastening note. "Mildred told me she'd smoke if she wanted to," Maryana had said. "She hadn't decided yet, but if she wanted to, she would."

I pressed *play*.

"One of Wanda's friends was givin' a party," Elliot's recorded voice was saying, "and she didn't invite Mildred. And I thought that wasn't right. So I called Mildred and asked her if she'd go to the movies with me. And she said, 'Elliott, I heard what happened, that I didn't get invited to Penny's party. I appreciate you takin' me to the movies.'"

I replayed that section, typing carefully, then fast-forwarded through the next patch, where I seemed to be doing all the talking. When I hit *play* again Elliott was saying, "—reminded me about Mildred's personality."

I rewound the tape. "Something you said reminded me about Mildred's personality." I rewound further, wondering why I didn't remember what had sprung that quote.

On the tape, Elliott asked me if I wanted to have children. I heard myself say that I did but not yet, there were still too many things I wanted to do.

Dorothy's house was quiet now. I stared at Birddog, Tom Sawyer and Indian Brave, then turned and looked into Tommy's blue pastel eyes.

Was that true?

I stayed in bed until I knew I wouldn't sleep, then gathered what I needed and went downstairs, leaving a note for Dorothy on the kitchen table. The route I'd mapped took me past my mother's grammar school and onto Stone Drive, where Dub had his dental office. I cut south, skirting the blank squares of the INDUSTRIAL AREA near the river, and got onto the highway that connected Kingsport, in the northeastern tip of the state, to Memphis, stuck in the lower left corner of my map like a wad of bubblegum. Halfway between the two lay Nashville, and below it, one-inch-equals-twenty-miles south, circled in red pen— Franklin, Tennessee.

Headlights ballooned in the rearview mirror. I braced for the vacuum pull of the big rigs, releasing my breath each time the silver silhouettes of dewlap pin-ups flapped past at eye level. My mother brought me to Tennessee every summer so I would know where my people came from, Marjorie Taylor had told me. But what did I know about this place? I couldn't name the crops poking through the rust-colored clay dirt, or the trees covering the hills, or the wildflowers scattered on the fields. My mother's friends talked about dogwoods in bloom and redbuds fading and dozens of plant species I couldn't even remember, much less identify. *Pink magnolias* was about as far as I'd get without a guidebook.

Like her friends, my mother had loved her garden. She'd spend hours in our backyard with her hands in the dirt. Why didn't she ask me to help?

Why didn't she show me the duplex she'd shared with Dorothy?

Why not take me to her schoolyard? Page through her year-book with me? Share a memory of her high school sweetie?

Or tell me about my grandmother standing on varicose legs at a sales counter in J. C. Penney.

Or tell me one fucking thing about Henry.

I didn't think I'd ever been this angry at her when she was alive.

And she didn't paint me, I thought, lighting a cigarette from the embers of another. She made a portrait of her best friend's son, but not so much as a sketch of her own daughter.

Why bring me to Tennessee and not tell me about it?

Why bring me out of her body and not tell me about her life?

I smoked and drove. Smoked and thought about my mother. Maybe the point was: She left all this. Maybe the point was that she was the one girl from Miz Hurt's art classes who'd used her skills to *get out*. Everything I remembered about Tennessee and everything I was learning now and everything I would never know about this place and her life here—she walked away from all of it.

She wanted things she didn't think she'd find here.

Okay.

I took the Nashville bypass and drove into Franklin under a cloudless sky. Not yet 10:00 A.M. but every bit of eighty degrees. The storefronts on Main Street had handsome awnings and simply lettered signs that looked made to code. I passed an obelisk with a military figure on top. Slowing, I read OUR CONFEDERATE SOLDIERS—part of an inscription wrapped around the base. I was pretty sure the rest of the phrase wasn't DIED TO KEEP SLAVES IN CHAINS.

Following directions I'd scribbled in my weekly planner, I took Hillsboro Road the last few miles, pulling onto the road's shoulder by a large wooden sign set in a clearing. A cloud of dirt sailed from under Dub's car toward the words HARRIS SCHOOL OF ART. I turned off the engine. From somewhere in the trees shading a large brick house, a lawnmower revved and settled into gear. A shaggy-haired young man came into view, pushing a mower around the shaggy yard. I wondered if the art school's students lived in the house—it looked big enough to have six or seven bedrooms upstairs. Or maybe there was a back building, a dorm.

birds— *mower*— I wrote in my notebook. I tried to picture the girl from the yearbook walking down the driveway on a bright spring morning like this. Sketch pad under one arm. Headed into the wooded hills across the road.

sun rises behind school—
morning light on the hills—
creek runs under the road—
smell—smoke, oniony grass, lilacs—

We had a lilac bush in Evanston. My mother took cuttings and spread bouquets around downstairs, filling our house with lilac perfume.

I closed my notebook, started the car and pulled onto the driveway. The shaggy kid pushing the mower was lost in the rhythms plugged into his ears. When no one answered at the front door I walked around the house, hoping this wasn't one of those country places where snarling dogs pop out like buckshot.

Lying near a tree, panting, an old shepherd with a white muzzle turned his frosted eyes in my direction. He didn't move or bark, so I had a moment to watch the small woman in a blue sweatsuit pour dog food into an aluminum bowl.

"Mrs. Harris?"

She pivoted, then stood. "Beth," she said, coming over with an outstretched hand. She was about the age I remembered my grandmother, and compact like Nellie Lady, but even at twenty paces I could see that Beth Harris was a different type of smallish seventyish Southern woman—different from the grandmother I remembered, and different from the grandmothers I'd been talking with since I got to Tennessee.

"You made good time," she said as we shook hands. No accent. Brown eyes clear as the water tumbling in the roadside creek.

"Couldn't sleep," I said, feeling exhausted, feeling elated. "I'm so glad to be here. My mother never told me she went to art school. I only found out about your school a couple weeks ago."

Those quick brown eyes studied me. "The Harris School was in Nashville when your mother was a student," she said.

"Ah." So I could toss my tender creekside notes.

"We were on Belmont Boulevard," she said, "across from Belmont College. We had three big buildings, all in old houses. When your mother was in school, we just had two buildings. We bought the third one the year after she graduated. But they're all down now—Belmont College tore them down and put up their own."

She started across the yard, away from the house and the dog. "Come," she said, and I followed along a beaten path toward an aluminum-sided building, thinking we were heading to the dorm.

"Isaac Harris opened his school in 1932," she was saying over the clatter of the lawnmower, "and I came to the school in 1936. We married three years later. Isaac was forty-three. I was twenty-three."

We'd reached the building. "I have something for you," she said, opening the door.

Not a dormitory but a studio, with works in progress on a dozen easels. In front was a long chalkboard covered with anatomically parsed figures. A framed painting of dancing couples in moonlight hung beside a charcoal composition of a cook in saggy toque with a spoon to his mouth. Clay skulls on a desktop took hollow-eyed measure of the scene.

"Isaac was born in 1895," Beth Harris said as we swept past the easels and chalkboard and skulls. More on Isaac, World War I vet, blah-blah, all of it going into my notebook because note-taking was a habit, because *she had something for me,* and I was try-ing to stay calm. Was another of my mother's artworks coming to me?

She opened a door and flicked the light and now my heartbeat became a nuisance. The room was larger than my half-a-shack in Newport Beach, its perimeter lined with file cabinets. The newer cabinets were here by the door, the older ones with rusted shins in back.

Beth Harris walked to the back of the room and opened a file drawer. I watched her fingers dance down a line of tabs. She pulled out a folder the color of milky coffee and brought it to me. It was an inch thick. The typed label on its third-cut tab was taped in place: MILDRED LADY 1945.

I opened to the first page, a pencil drawing of a purple flower I couldn't name in a spray of feathery ferns. The second page was a childish sketch of a smiling piggy bank standing among scattered coins. "An Empty Stomach" was written in decorative cursive across the bottom. Third page—

"That was one of the drawings your mother sent in with her application," Beth Harris said.

We stared at the portrait of a dark-eyed young man with Bryl-creemed hair and upturned coat collar. A young Bogart type, skillfully etched and limned and smudged to life. He was beauti-ful. It was beautiful. I could hardly breathe.

"Your mother had a lot of talent," she said. "I feel like I've been keeping this all these years so I could give it to you."

I tore my gaze from Bogey. "You're the second person who's said that to me. The other one gave me two of her paintings."

"You need these things for your soul."

"That's kind of how I think of it, too," I said.

The mower had stopped and the old dog had fallen asleep when we got back outside. Beth Harris ushered me through her comfortably cluttered rooms, and it was enough for me just to see her overstuffed bookshelves and upright piano piled with music, her lightly chafed antiques and walls crammed with paintings and drawings like those in the studio. I didn't need to take notes. I had my mother's file in my shoulder bag—one inch equals four years of art school. Every few minutes I reached in and touched the chamois-soft folder to make sure it hadn't slipped away.

We sat in the kitchen, making a place for sweaty glasses of iced tea and plates of sliced fruit in a still-life jumble of unopened mail and art supplies. I prompted her through a brief tour of her childhood in Texas and Florida. She mentioned that she'd trained at the Art Institute of Chicago.

"How did you like the Art Institute school?" I asked.

"I couldn't stand it!" she said. "It was just *awful.* That's true with most art schools. This may sound strange to you, but most art schools don't teach anything. They just assume you're born as an artist and you don't have to learn."

"That's funny."

"My first class in composition, the teacher said, 'Bring in a composition that has three people on a staircase.' I couldn't draw people. I couldn't draw a staircase. I couldn't draw *anything,*" she said, and we both laughed.

When her parents divorced, she followed her father to Nashville, where she "opened the telephone book and on the first page it said, 'Advertising Art School.' That's what it was called when your mother was a student, too."

Beth not-yet-Harris had enrolled at the Advertising Art School just five years before my mom, and by sophomore year was an assistant teacher. After she married the boss she continued to teach, expanding the program to include out-of-town students by offering dorm living in her own home.

"We lived downstairs," she said, "and the girls used the five big bedrooms upstairs, three girls to a room."

"So it was a girls' school?"

"When your mother came, in 1941, we had as many boys as

girls. But when the war happened we lost all the boys. So from 'forty-two and all during the war, when your mother was here, we had all girls."

"What kind of a student was my mother?"

Beth Harris took a long drink of tea. "Your mother was a very hard worker and an excellent student," she said, putting down her glass. "She kept to herself mostly. We had school five days a week and on the weekends the students could do anything they wanted. They could go home, or they could go visit somebody, or they could stay and work. It was very casual around the school—they wore blue jeans and T-shirts, and in the summertime they wore shorts, halters, bathing suits if they wanted to. And during the war years was the most beautiful thing. We had marvelous times. The girls walked down to what was called Hillsboro Village—it was kind of bohemian, in the university area, with Vanderbilt right there, and Peabody, and everybody going down there to tea rooms and chocolate shops and beer places. And we always had parties and dances and a big masquerade ball."

"Sounds like fun."

"That was the best part of my life," she said. "It was never the same after the boys came back. We got another building for the boys' dormitory, but the clashes started—the battle of the sexes. And the marriages. It was called the Advertising Art School but then I started calling it the Agonizing Hearts School."

She left the kitchen and returned with a framed black-and-white studio portrait. "That's Isaac when he was eighty-two. He died that year."

"Very handsome."

"The sad thing was that Isaac didn't want to marry me in the first place," she said, a smile softening her words. "I wanted to marry him, and I wanted the school to grow, with the dorms and all the rest. Poor Isaac just wanted to teach and have his own private life. He didn't want to marry a girl who was so much younger. He did love me, and I loved him, but he didn't think he'd be a good husband because he couldn't have children. He kept saying, 'You want children, and I can't have 'em. You should marry someone else.' And I'd say, 'No. I don't want anybody but you.' "

We looked at the photograph. I said, "That's romantic."

"It was, but it was sad, too. He went along with everything I wanted, and it was too much for him. He hung in there, and he was lovely about it. But it wasn't what he wanted. I can see that now," she said. "Now that he's gone."

I'm going to tell you this because I think you need to hear it for your own peace of mind," Beth Harris said. We were standing on the back porch, near where I'd first seen her four hours earlier. I'd packed away my cassette and notebook. I thought we were saying goodbye.

"I feel very close to you now," she said. "I do."

"I'm glad we met." I reached into my bag and touched my mother's file. She watched my hand. Then her fox eyes fixed on me as if I were a model in a life-studies class.

"They didn't like her," she said abruptly.

"Who didn't?"

"*I* liked her," she said, "as a student. She was a good student, and I liked her for that purpose. And she had talent and she loved art. She worked hard and I admired that. But she was very selfish, and hardly anybody liked her."

"Okay."

"She'd get boxes from home and she didn't ever share them. Boxes of cookies and jam and all kinds of things. She'd get a box and take it into her room and eat it by herself. And the other girls got so angry at her they played a rotten trick on her."

"What happened?"

"I could see why they did it, but I thought it was wrong."

"What was wrong?"

"They got real mad at her one time, and they made up a box and acted like it was sent to one of them. And they put all this rotten stuff in it!"

She laughed. So did I.

"See, they put one of their names on the box, and put it out where she would grab something and eat it. The girl who thought of it wanted *vengeance.* The other girls went along because they thought it was funny."

"What was in the box?"

"I can't remember all of it, but one thing I remember particularly was that they made something with soap powder, made it like it was a spread to put on bread."

"Did she eat it?"

"Yes! And they came to me and told me about it, and they were just dyin' laughin', and I had to say, 'This is terrible.' I said, 'If you make her sick you all will be in trouble.' I told them you don't do this to people. 'Suppose she dies,' I said. 'Suppose it was poison.' And they said, 'It's not going to kill her.' "

I'd been staring at the gnarled old tree where the old dog had lain when I arrived, his dirt patch and food bowl empty now. I turned to the art teacher in her blue sweatsuit. "Did she get sick from it?"

"The miracle was, she didn't."

"Do you remember which year that was?"

"That was her first year," Beth Harris said, her gaze locked on mine. "I never did understand your mother. It was frustrating because I wanted to love her, and I couldn't. And the students couldn't either. Mildred wasn't like anybody I've ever known. I thought about her for years and years."

*Y*ou *were a beauty*, I typed, and listened to the Smith-Corona's electric hum. The Indian Brave had a knife on his hip and feathers in his shiny black braids. Tom Sawyer's eyes were blue smears trained on a leaf-dashed sky. Birddog held my stare.

You were a beauty, I read, and typed, *In my newly sentimental view. I probably have a hundred pictures of you now—of you then. I have them now. They're mine. I have baby you on your daddy's knee and in your mother's arms. Studio portraits of you as you grew. Snaps of you with your school friends, your church friends, in your band uniform, in summer dresses, horseback riding on the Farm. And here's the kicker: I have a picture of you and Henry and Nellie together by the sun-bleached shingles of a house in Newport Beach. How about that. You're wearing black pants and a ruffled bathing suit top and white Keds. You're sitting on a low wooden fence next to Henry. Nellie stands by his side, about the same height as him sitting. I know from the date written on the back that you're twenty-five. I know from a cousin of yours who gave me the photograph—peeled it off a black construction-paper page in her photo album and put it in my trembling hand—that you and Henry and Nellie took a train trip west to visit Nellie's brothers and sisters in California. As the shutter closed you looked at Henry, shielding your eyes under his fedora's brim, and the wind lashed your hair across your cheek.*

"Trembling hand"—I just reread. See what happens? My hands tremble, my heart pounds. I'm swimming in clichés.

Women tend the photo albums. That's one thing I've learned here. Women fill their houses with photographs of their mothers and grandmothers—and their children. Only a woman would think to save her baby's curls in a candy box. Men may rule their lives, but in memory women cling to their mothers. And their children.

At night Dorothy sits in an armchair under a fading picture of her mother in her wedding dress. I got a double whammy at your cousin Helen Stone's house: Helen sits under a picture of her parents on their wedding day, and when I commented on it—I remember Aunt Grace so well from our visits—Helen jumped up and got a silver-framed photo of her daughter Tina, and held it up by the picture of Grace. What could I say about a daughter getting married in her grandmother's wedding dress?

One of your church friends gave me a brown scrap of newsprint from 1950—you in floor-length white satin and cap, hands tucked into a small bouquet. So now I have my mom's wedding picture, too.

My hands pound, my heart trembles.

I went to the Farm. A highway cuts through the property now. Juanita keeps busy with a little herd of Black Angus and a big vegetable garden. She feeds her cats and cleans the house and mows acres of lawn— and she learned to drive not long ago, like Dorothy after Roy died. Juanita drives to a local school to cook lunch for the kids.

Aunt Lily died first, then Uncle Riley. Arch died the day his brother Andrew was buried. Most of the rest of the dead Juanita told me about I only remember as names.

I stayed at the Farm for a couple weeks, driving around Rock Springs and Double Springs and Fall Branch in your cousin Dub's car, talking to this one and that one, same as in town. I took notes and transcribed tapes and gathered my study aids. Every day I walked down the gravel driveway, past a pond cut in half by a highway, and followed the old road under the new viaduct to the Double Springs Missionary Baptist Church. New sign. New parking lot. Same old little white church.

You brought me there so you could wander among the graves. Now I know why. I found all the Ladys in the lower churchyard, then followed the fence up to the Ladys at the top of the hill. I know some of the stories that go with the old-timers' names now. I found an Elizabeth Lady who lived a hundred years ago and wondered if your middle name honored her. I met a Mildred in Kingsport who claims you as her namesake—

didn't like her much. Don't like the name Mildred much, either. And now that I know more about you, I don't think it fits. When you were a kid, trying to learn how to paint, you signed your canvases with your initials, MEL, and that's how I've started to think of you. The nickname suits you, at least the part of your story written in Tennessee—birth certificate to art school grad. Helluva first act, Mel. Much better than mine. You drew a future for yourself and climbed in.

Up there among the hilltop Ladys, I spent hours by the big dark stone inscribed with the names and dates of Henry's parents. Their last surviving child, your Aunt Mandy, told me that her father went to his barn every morning and got down on his knees and prayed. I thought about that as I sat in the graveyard. I tried to imagine William Melvin Lady and Nettie Bruner Lady, their hard lives and seven children and the farms they scraped together that were swallowed by Henry's debts. Your grandparents lived into their eighties and died the same year, which might make their single headstone a practical choice, a money saver. Or maybe, I started thinking, after all they'd been through together—all those children to take care of, all those acres to plant and plow, all those farm animals to get what could be gotten from between birth and slaughter—endless, endless chores—maybe William Melvin and Nettie Bruner Lady were buried under one headstone in memory of their twined lives, poetically.

Maybe.

I'm going North now. You went North. Funny how your people talk about your husband. They don't say much, of course, but when I rewind my tapes and listen closely I think I know what they mean. Your cousin Denzel, Andrew's son, told me Allan asked to borrow $25,000 from Andrew one summer in the sixties. A few days later I asked Dub, offhandedly, if Allan ever tried to borrow money from Arch, and Dub named the same year and the same amount. Dorothy's older son, Toby, remembered Allan giving him a silver money clip as a birthday present. My favorite was Helen Stone. Helen's as bubbly and chatty as ever, and we'd talked for hours before she mentioned Allan. "I understand your father was of another faith," she said.

W ell I just can't believe you're leaving us," Dorothy said. She was at the kitchen table, reading the *Kingsport Times-News.*

"It does kind of seem like I moved in," I said, crossing behind her. Four duct-taped book boxes were stacked by the screen door, beside the portable typewriter and suitcase I'd arrived with seven weeks ago. I added two new carry-on bags to the pile. "Look at all this stuff," I said. "Jim better bring a U-Haul."

"Well, now, Jim called a little while ago. I guess he's got a meeting at the bank that's come up at the last minute. He said to tell you he was real sorry."

"That's okay." I poured a cup of coffee. "I'll just get a cab. Only horrible people make you take them to the airport, anyway."

Dorothy's expression was mock shock. This was our Clash of the Cultures routine—brash vs. gracious. Big City vs. Small Town. Yankee bull in a Southern china shop.

"Bruce is comin' by to get you," she said. "I called him while you were in the shower."

"That's crazy."

"It's not *crazy,* Pamela."

"You're forcing me to freeload till the moment I leave?"

"Well I guess I am."

"Dorothy—really—I should take a cab."

"Oh law. You know what that'd run you? Bruce will take you out there, now. It'll give him a little break."

I couldn't argue with that. Bruce needed a break. On one of my first days in Kingsport, Dorothy had driven us to her brother's house. As she cautiously maneuvered quiet streets to the other side of town, she prepared me to meet her sister-in-law, who'd had cancer and a stroke. Bruce opened the door and led us to a dark sitting room where his wife sat wrapped in blankets, chain-smoking as she watched TV, flicking her ashes in the general direction of an end table loaded with cigarettes, tissues, medicine.

"What's the program at church today?" I asked Dorothy now, scanning a front page headlined U.S. SHIPS BLAST IRANIAN OIL FACILITIES.

"It's a travelogue about Hawaii."

"If you see Vera Ruth and the Taylors and the others, please tell them goodbye for me." I took a sip of coffee. "I won't wait twenty years to come back this time."

"Well I hope not," Dorothy said.

CONTROVERSIAL GASOLINE BILL SPARKS BATTLE. "I guess it was ten years," I said.

"You still don't remember your grandmother's funeral, do you?"

"Not really. No."

Dorothy carried her cup to the sink. "Did you get a chance to go up to Oak Hill?"

Before I could answer, Bruce came booming through the screen door. "Chauffeur's here!" He pointed at my to-go pile. "You takin' all this back to California?"

"I'm sending the boxes home," I said, "and taking the rest to Chicago."

"*Chicago?*"

"Pamela's going to see her dad," Dorothy said. The Yankee bull decided to sidestep that bit of china and load the car. Then I hugged Dorothy, holding on to her for a few extra beats, as I had when I'd arrived. Then we were off.

"Can I ask a small favor?" I said, as Bruce turned onto Wanola.

"Another one?"

"Ha." I pulled out my town map.

"What are you lookin' for?"

"Oak Hill Cemetery," I said.

He glanced over. "You want to go up there *now?*"

"Just for a minute. Here it is." I pointed to the map. "Look how close it is."

Bruce shook his head and drove off in silence. Ten minutes later, atop a hill due north of Dorothy's, we passed through the cemetery's iron gates. Bruce parked.

"This will only take a minute," I said, and hurried to the office. The clerk wrote down my information and went to her files, returning with a map and a note: "Section D, Lot 121."

Section D was on a slope. Nearing the crest I saw the wide upright stone, L A D Y, in a patch of dandelions and brown turf. The first marker I stepped up to was a surprise.

VIRGINIA R. LADY

APR. 5, 1926

APR. 11, 1926

An hour later, Bruce and I were at Tri-Cities Airport. He'd taken me to a shipping store, where I'd left my boxes, and now we stood outside the terminal with the rest of my luggage on a baggage cart.

"I just have one question," he said, wiping his brow with a rumpled handkerchief. "Do you try to tell it straight, or do you put a slant on things?"

I laughed. "I used to have an answer for that."

"You know what I mean."

"I do. It's a good question. I'll have to get back to you on that one, Bruce."

My flight was boarding when I got to the gate. I dug out my Week-At-a-Glance and hurried to a pay phone. A thin voice answered after many rings.

"Virgie?" I said.

"Who's 'at?"

"It's Henry and Nellie Lady's granddaughter."

"Well hey there, honey! We's just talkin' 'bout you the other day." She turned from the phone, *"It's Mildred Lady's girl,"* I heard her say, and I pictured the two of them, Virgie and John Cox— Sugar and Daddy—with the receiver between their two white heads.

"I want to thank you again for giving me that yearbook," I said. "I'm so glad to have it."

"You down at Dorothy's now?"

"I'm at the airport, actually. I'm leaving today. I just had one more thing—one question."

"What's 'at?"

"Do you remember my grandmother having a second child? A baby girl that only lived a few days?"

"Virginia Ruth," Virgie said.

R for Ruth. "Yes. What happened to her?"

"Had the spinal meningitis. Missus Lady must have had her at home, 'cause I remember it like to kill her."

"Almost killed my grandmother."

"Uh-huh."

"The birth did."

"No, not like that. Like to broke her heart."

It was late afternoon when the cab from O'Hare got to Helen's parents' house in Evanston. I unloaded my bags at the curb and stayed there for a minute, admiring a house I'd visited hundreds of times but never really looked at before. Shadows from the pine trees out front dappled the stucco and splashed across the tile roof. Looking north, toward Main Street, I mentally navigated to the big white house on the corner of Forest and Greenleaf. Was it five blocks from here? Six?

I collected my luggage and went around back. The house keys were in a flowerpot, as promised. Leaving bags and typewriter in the kitchen, I went looking for the cat that was my excuse for a week's free lodging.

"Here Spook!" I called, wandering the familiar rooms. Helen Rosenberg and I had been friends since kindergarten at Lincoln Elementary School, on Main. She was the one classmate I'd kept in touch with in the late seventies, when the kids I'd grown up with were passing through the larval stages of middle-class suburbanites everywhere—off to college, home for holidays, out into the white-collar workforce with a safety net back at the ol' homestead. The track I'd been on till I suddenly wasn't. This summer Helen and I would both turn thirty, and we were back in step for that final pivot away from childhood. She had just taken a children's librarian job in L.A. I was a short shot down the 405 freeway in Newport Beach. Usually I was.

"Here Spook!"

I stopped by the shawl-draped piano in the living room. The

shelves behind it were filled with books in German. There was a music stand nearby, an instrument case next to its spindly legs. Helen's parents, both German immigrants, played duets on flute and piano. I pictured them together here, filling their empty nest with the Brahms sonata on the music stand.

Wandering upstairs, I remembered that it wasn't until we were in high school that Helen learned what had happened to her parents during World War II. Her mom had told her, as they sorted laundry one day, about being sent to England as a teen to escape the Nazis—and never seeing her own mother again. "And your dad was in a camp," Mrs. Rosenberg said, in the accented English that Helen perfectly mimicked. "He doesn't ever talk about it, but he still has nightmares."

I was in my friend's old bedroom, where the hippie decor had been distilled to a lonely Stones poster and a macramé web, when I noticed a black cat watching me from the windowsill. Coaxing Spook downstairs, I filled a bowl with Kibbles and picked up the phone.

"The Eagle has landed," I said when Kevin answered.

"That's one giant leap for you, darlin'."

"Ha."

"Everything okay?"

I looked around the kitchen, recalling the night Helen and I baked dope brownies and invited over everyone we knew. Her parents were away then, too. "It's pretty weird to be here."

"Maybe you should go to a hotel."

"I haven't made a nickel in two months."

"We don't care about that," Kevin said. "If you want to go, go. Get a neighbor to feed the cat."

"It's not the cat. It's . . . *Chicagoland*," I said, using the local term for the suburbs. "It's full of ghosts."

"I wish I were there."

"My mom had a baby sister who only lived a few days," I said.

"Whoa. Did Dorothy tell you that?"

"I saw her grave this morning. She's buried with my grandparents."

"That's rough."

"Then I called Allan from Charlotte. I had some time to kill between planes."

"How's he doing?"

"He's busy," I said. "He's a busy businessman. I heard about all the plans he has this week—lunches, dinners, some wedding they're going to."

"You'll get your time with him."

"It's not like I asked to crash with them or anything. Which wouldn't be the most bizarre request, would it? I mean, I'm in Chicago, my father lives in Chicago, and I have to scramble a house-sit."

"You don't want to stay with Allan and Judy."

"Too true. But you know what? This just kind of jumps out at me, on my little quest here: I go to my mother's hometown— everybody wants to help. I come to *my* hometown—I call *my father*—and I get blown off."

Kevin sighed. "The point is that you're there, and you get what you need."

"The point is he's an asshole."

"Just don't tell him that."

I set up shop in the breakfast room, placing my typewriter and files on the table so I could work with a view of the backyard. I took bubblewrap off my mother's paintings and stood them on a radiator facing my chair. I had four small canvases now—a cousin of my mother's had pulled one from her attic a few days ago and given it to me. It was a picture of a black kitten on a blue tablecloth, stalking a bee hovering by a vase of flowers. The palette matched the others from art class at Miz Hurt's. I sat behind my typewriter and stared at my treasures, thinking about the girl who'd painted them.

Thinking about Mel, as she was still signing her work when she came to live among the Yankees.

She was twenty-two years old when she got to Chicago. It was 1945. I'd found the address of her first apartment in Beth Harris's coffee-colored file, below the pencil sketches Mildred Lady submitted with her art school application, below a chronology of report cards and tuition bills and perfunctory correspondence between the school and my grandparents. The address was on a yellowed envelope at the bottom of the file. *Dear Professor and Mrs. Harris,* the letter inside began. *I'm here now and almost settled. The place is wonderful, the people nicer than I'd hoped . . .*

Hard to read. Hard for me even to touch, to hold. The presence of the young woman in her dashed-off words was as startling to me as the first glimpse of my mother in a dream six months ago.

Dorothy had been the key in Kingsport, my link to a chain of my mother's friends and acquaintances. Without Dorothy, all I'd have of Mildred Lady's first twenty-two years would be dry stats on public records and impressions of places that had changed since my mother's time in ways I couldn't know.

In Chicago, I realized, my father would have to be my guide.

"She didn't have friends here," I told Indian Brave, Tom Sawyer, Birddog and Kitten. Except Frankie, I thought. And Frankie was dead.

I thought about the day my father drove me and my brother to the southside for Frankie's funeral. It must have been before he went bankrupt, because I could see us tooling down Lake Shore Drive in a big brown Benz. We'd been the only white people at the service. Frankie's husband Morris had wept in my father's arms. She'd had cancer, I remembered. Was it breast cancer?

I got up and paced the downstairs rooms.

When I returned to the table I spread out my files and started a list—a reporter's checklist—to keep the ghosts at bay.

—2410 N Lakeview

—624 S Michigan

—49 E Elm

Her first apartment. His ad agency. The townhouse they'd bought as newlyweds. I added places I'd been many times with my mother—the Art Institute, the Field Museum, Lincoln Park Zoo. I added my schools, our churches, Marshall Field's.

Why?

I sat and looked at the list, then tore it from the notebook and tossed it in the trash on my way out.

The front yards along Judson Avenue were filled with children playing at dusk. I turned onto Main and walked west, away from the lake, trying to picture the storefronts as they'd been twenty years before.

There was a clothes shop where the grocery store had been—so what?

Here was the bank my father had brought me to each time he added to my "college fund"—a thick stack of what must have been Treasury bills. I remembered the diplomalike sheaves stuffed in a long skinny safe-deposit box. He'd cashed them all before his debts sank him.

I passed under the crumbling stone viaduct where the el crossed Main, and stopped in front of Good's paint store. Mrs. Allan Marin had a charge account at Good's, and at Vogue Fabrics in the ugly brick building next door. Mrs. Allan Marin brought her young daughter and elderly mother to Good's and Vogue in a cab that waited, meter running, then took them home again.

We came here for the bubblegum-pink paint custom-mixed for my bedroom.

We came here for a pattern for hotpants when I was in junior high.

The stores were exactly as I remembered them. The buildings were exactly as they'd been. They told me: We're here. They said: She's gone.

And then passers-by were turning to look at the sobbing woman. One stopped to offer a tissue, but I waved her away. This was why I hadn't come here in the years I'd lived in Chicago, not even when I'd had an apartment in Rogers Park, no more than a mile away.

I walked back under the tracks, following Main past Lincoln Elementary School, and turned onto Forest Avenue. The block facing the schoolyard was filled with apartment buildings. Crossing Lee Street, which gave its name to the beach a few streets east, I stepped onto our block.

Past Liz Halsted's—she'd been my best friend till she moved away after fourth grade.

Past the Kennedys'—Susan Kennedy went horseback riding with me.

The Swedish handyman lived in this one. Next door had been the Ericksons', where a dozen or more of us kids met on summer nights to pick teams for cops and robbers.

Oscar Mayer, the cold-cuts king, had lived in this stone mansion, his side yard filling a space large enough for another home. Every now and then we'd see the Oscar Mayer Weinermobile parked out front, its pink hot-dog ends curling like a smile from its tan bun-chassis.

At the corner of Forest and Greenleaf, I sat with my back to the house where a girl named Suzy had lived. Suzy was in my class at Lincoln but never came out to play cops and robbers with us on summer nights. I looked across Forest at the big white house with two-story Corinthian columns. Ten-forty-seven-Forest Avenue-Evanston-Illinois. I could move through its rooms, as in my dreams. I could see us.

"Your life was good when you were younger," Dorothy had said.

But how could it have been? I was gone when my mother came home. Why did she go to California, anyway? Where did she stay?

She'd been away for months—I didn't know how long. That time was a blank. And no one told me she was coming home. No one told me anything.

I had asked to go to my friend Laura's farm that weekend. My father said fine. And when Laura's father dropped me off on Sunday night and I saw the porch light on and the house dark I knew something was wrong.

Where was everybody?

But I knew.

I came through the front door and saw my grandmother at the top of the stairs in her nightgown, her cheeks wet with tears, and I started yelling. *Where is she? What happened?* I ran upstairs and went straight into their room—my mother had been there. The cover was pulled back on her side of the bed. The sheets were bunched where she'd been, a frozen lake.

I woke to my father's voice on the answering machine. I'd fallen asleep in the living room, under an Indian-print blanket from Helen's bed. I rolled off the couch and hurried to the kitchen.

"I'm here," I said, picking up.

"Well good morning, dear. I hope I'm not disturbing you."

"I was in the other room."

"I thought we could go for a little drive this morning," he said. "I've got a place in mind for lunch."

"Sure." Eight-twenty on the stove clock. I was still in the clothes I'd put on yesterday under the pastel gaze of Dorothy's middle son. "I thought you had a wedding to go to or something."

"There's been a change of plan."

I was on the front steps, hair drip-drying in the sun, when my father's brown Corolla came up the street an hour later. Same little car he'd had since the last of the Benzes went poof eleven years ago. I'd asked to borrow the Corolla once, I remembered. I must have been nineteen or twenty. I knew he let his girlfriend drive it downstate to visit her family.

"Can't do it," he'd said.

"Why not? Judy drives it."

Insurance, he'd said. His insurance didn't cover me. I felt a little flare of ancient anger at the memory as I watched my father haul himself stiffly from the bucket seat and come around the bumper with a limp. He was wearing a yellow polo shirt tucked into pressed jeans. The broad shoulders and thick chest that had seemed to add to his modest stature now supported a round gut. I hadn't seen him since Thanksgiving, six months ago.

"You look thin," he said, as we embraced. He stepped back, holding my upper arms.

"I *am* thin," I said, forcing a smile. He was seventy-five years old. And limping—his knees had given him trouble for years. But I wouldn't ask about that. Questions about his health were usually answered in terms of the "good work" he was doing, meaning, as I understood Christian Science jargon, that he was thinking good thoughts to make a bad thing go away.

When we were buckled in, I said, "How's Judy?"

"She works too hard," he said, and then he gave me the spiel, which was why I'd asked. He always seemed to enjoy telling me that Judy was overworked, she was underpaid, and that boss of hers, Jesus, you'd think he'd make her a partner . . .

Judy was a travel agent. When they'd begun dating I'd felt an immense gulf between my seventeen years and her thirty-three. Now that I was twenty-nine to her forty-five I could see her more clearly, and understand her less.

He turned left on Main, drove two blocks to the corner by the bank and made a right onto Chicago Avenue. An el train rattled along the tracks. We were heading north, toward Greenleaf Street, but we wouldn't pass our house. My father had put three blocks between us and Forest Avenue.

"Judy will be working long after I'm pushing up daisies," he was saying. The steeple of the First Baptist Church came into sight up ahead. Just beyond it were the stone columns of the Federal-style First Church of Christ, Scientist.

"It's kind of amazing that our churches were right next door to each other, isn't it?" I said as we passed them. "Is that why you and Mom picked Evanston?"

"That was happenstance," he said.

I wished I could see through his wraparound sunglasses. Had he glanced at the churches? Was he sneaking peeks at me? He made a left on Clark Street and we passed under the train tracks, skirting the edge of Northwestern University's campus. He made another turn and now we were heading west, away from the mansions by the lake.

But my thoughts were still snagged on the Baptist steeple. "So, when she found the house," I said, "I guess it was a pretty big bonus that your churches were next-door neighbors."

"I don't know if it was a 'bonus,' dear. That's your word. It was a *happenstance.*"

"And then splitting the kids—"

"Mildred and I made that arrangement before we ever considered moving to Evanston," he said. "She would go to the Baptist church with you and Nellie, and your brother and I would go to the Christian Science church. It was a fair division."

"I was just wondering—"

"And it was *clearly understood* before we got married, and while we were married, that you go to your church and I'll go to mine. I never tried to drag her into the Science church."

"Okay."

"*Never.*"

People do that in interviews all the time—they blurt. They answer a question they're afraid you'll ask, or one they want you to ask, before you get to it. Before you've even thought of it, sometimes. You can jump right in with follow-ups, and stir things up, or you can wait, and let the spilled beans simmer.

I looked past my father's stony profile as we crossed Dodge Avenue, to see if I could glimpse my high school. This was the way we'd driven to the stables for my Saturday-morning riding lessons when I was little, but once I got to high school and had a horse of my own to ride every day, I hitchhiked to the stables from school, or took a bus to Old Orchard Shopping Center and walked the last mile west on Golf Road. I never had a problem hitching, though the neighborhood around school wasn't the best. As we drove in silence, I thought that might have been because I'd walked away from as many cars as I'd gotten into. *Driver only* was the rule I'd made for myself. If I stuck my thumb out too close to school, a carload of trouble would inevitably pull over, and I'd bolt before it got to a stop.

"Fucking bitch!"—thrown at my back as tires squealed.

"Spread your legs, cunt!"

Emerson Street changed names as it passed through Skokie, becoming Golf Road at Crawford Avenue. I'd totaled one of my dad's cars at this corner. There was the gas station where I'd gone to call and tell him that his lovely gray Mercedes, his first Benz after a string of Cadillacs and Lincolns, was sitting in the rain, in the dark, with smoke streaming from its crushed grille.

We passed the polo field where I used to let Helluva Note gallop at the end of our trail rides. My father turned right at Harms Road, and now I knew where we were going. A mile north on Harms was Hackney's, a little black box of a restaurant tucked among the houses facing the forest preserve.

We ate on the patio, where I prompted my father through tales of his latest trip to the Bahamas. Judy sent him on solo jaunts every thirteen weeks. He stayed in the same room at the same hotel, sunbathed, swam, slept. "Recharging my batteries," he called it.

"That was very nice, dear," he said, as we finished lunch. *"Très agréable."*

"Have you got a little more time?"

"What do you have in mind?"

"A few questions," I said. I pointed to the picnic grounds at the edge of the forest preserve. "Maybe we could sit in there?"

A barbecue for a gathering of what looked like one large overstuffed family was taking shape by the preserve's nearest parking lot. We passed the paper-draped tables, blaring boom box, a tree festooned with streamers. We left the car in the next lot and walked to a picnic table half in sunlight, half in shadow.

My father sat at the bright end with his elbows behind him on the tabletop and his wraparounds tipped to the sun. The close-cropped fringe circling his tanned pate was white, but the fur on his arms was still inky black.

I sat on the shady side and put my cassette between us. I'd made a few notes for the interview, and I opened my notebook. He glanced at my setup, looked away.

"So I learned a lot in Tennessee," I said, pressing the *record* button. No reaction. I let a minute of birdsong and traffic sounds fill the tape.

"I guess she came up to Chicago right after graduating from art school," I said. Would it interest him that I knew about my mother's alma mater? We'd never spoken of it before.

"She didn't talk much about art school," he told the sky.

"You know her first apartment was near a place I lived? On Lakewood, near Fullerton."

"I don't know about that." Maybe he was watching me, behind his dark lenses.

"Why don't we start with when you met," I said. "Do you remember the day?"

"Of course I remember it. I've written a chapter about Mildred."

Right. Kevin had mentioned that a "chapter" had arrived while I was in Tennessee. It suddenly occurred to me that my father might have written about my mom *because* I'd gone to Tennessee. Was that what this stonewalling was all about? Were we in some kind of biographical pissing match here?

"Mildred came up to Chicago in September of 'forty-five," he said, breaking the silence.

"Is that when you met?"

"No, dear. Are you telling this, or am I?"

"You are," I said. "Sorry."

He shifted his weight. "I was married to Betty Jacobson at the time. Betty Susan Jacobson Marin Spitz Bennett—those are all her names now. Betty was thin, blond and beautiful. Really a classic beauty."

Sometime after my mother died—sometime when I was still in my teens—my father had made a comment about "Betty" that led to my discovery that my mom was his second wife. The news hadn't mattered then, or maybe it was too much for me to take in at the time, and I'd half forgotten it. Now I asked him about his first wife, and he described a spoiled rich girl who'd dropped out of UCLA and was living with her parents in Chicago when he met her. Details tumbled out—about her up-by-the-bootstraps father, Isador, the auto-supply stores he owned with his partner Ragnet, Betty's lovely younger sister, her parents' lavish home in Hyde Park, near the University of Chicago, my father's alma mater. Since he was rolling, I drew him back through the high-light reel from his prep school days in Chicago and Milwaukee to his golden years at college. Robert Hutchins, the university's fabled president, and his Great Books course had been staples at our Sunday lunch table, along with tales of my grandfather Jacob Marin, the hard-working tailor from Alsace-Lorraine. Jacob had given his children the best education the New World had to offer.

After graduating from the U. of C. in 'thirty-four, my father took a job with a patent medicine company.

"Really?" I said, a twelve-year-old's follow-up.

"Yes, dear, *really*."

Odd job for a Christian Scientist, I thought, but kept that to myself. He told me about an "old-line, direct-mail patent medicine company" founded in 1869.

"When I arrived on the scene, the business had dropped from its peak of $2 million in sales to about $400,000," he said. "And the reason for that is we sold our product to foreigners, and restrictive immigration was put in in 1921, so our market was shrinking."

"Why sold to foreigners?"

"That was the background of the company, dear."

"I mean, were they thought to be more gullible?" Baiting him. Regressing. Wisely, he ignored the question. "So what was in the 'medicine'?" I asked.

"We called it by different names in different languages."

"But what was it?"

"We called it a 'stomactic tonic.' "

"What was in it?"

"It was fourteen percent alcohol in a senna tea base. Actually, it was a laxative."

I moved on to a favored topic—his Air Force duty as a general's aide—and led him from Okinawa back to Chicago, through his divorce from the beautiful Betty and into the agency business with his brother, Leonard. One day, in 1948, a fledgling artist named Mildred Lady walked into Allan Marin & Associates with samples of her work.

"Her book was marvelous," he said, animated by the memory. "Just marvelous! The reason I wasn't terribly interested in her background as to schools—to get back to your first question—is because it was very obvious looking through Mildred's book that she had a tremendous flair for visualization."

He took off his sunglasses. The skin near his eyes was dotted with small dark moles. The larger freckles and age spots from seven decades of sunbathing were less noticeable on the rest of his ruddy face.

"Her particular forte was layouts," he said, "and she was a very fast worker. In my entire experience in the advertising business, I've never had such close and complete communication as I did working with Mildred. I could just mumble something, and it would become a reality."

He glanced over, handed me his handkerchief.

"There was a famous patent medicine guy from Louisiana," he continued without commenting on my tears. "Dudley LeBlanc. Jesus, what a character! Dudley LeBlanc was touring the country in a private train with Jack Dempsey, Carmen Miranda—people like that. He was putting on shows—at Wrigley Field, for example. And all you needed to get into the show was a box top from his product. Well, somehow I got hold of LeBlanc, and I told him I'd like to bring him some advertising ideas when he got to Chicago. And he said, *'Dat's fahn, cousin, dat's fahn!'* That telephone conversation took place on a Saturday night. I came back to the dinner table—I'd been so excited about this, I'd gotten up in the middle of dinner—and I said to Mildred, 'You want to do some patent medicine ads?' So we put together seven or eight full-page newspaper ads that night. And they absolutely floored LeBlanc!"

Patent medicine again?

"Let's go back for a moment," I said. "Let's go back to when she first came to the agency."

She was living on Elm Street, he told me, in a garret rented from a widow who often invited her down for dinner. "Mildred's apartment was really just one room," he said, "but a fairly good-sized room, and she kept it very tidy. She had her sleeping quarters in one section, and kind of a living room area with a dinky kitchen. And she had her drawing board in the bay window, facing Elm Street."

"What was on the drawing board?"

"Layouts for consumer ads and brochures."

"Did she do any painting?"

"She did paint some, yes. She did some oils. One of the paintings I remember was a self-portrait," he said. "It wasn't bad. It wasn't great. It was beyond just plain amateur talent. I think she had a desire at one point to be an artist, you know, in oils. A fine artist. But she wasn't good enough, and she realized that."

The shade had moved off our table and the sunlight made my notes unreadable. "Who were her favorite artists?" I asked.

"I don't recall any strong preferences," he said. "She followed the commercial artists whose work appeared in the *Saturday Evening Post*. And she had tremendous files of their work. Boxes and boxes of clippings."

In Tennessee, Maryana Smith Huff had told me that my mother returned from a year at art school with the news that artists needed picture files.

"And as I recall, she kept her sheet music in with her clippings," my father said. "These were things she played on the piano—church music, hymns, popular songs. She'd been collecting them for years."

"She played piano?" Her father Henry had hocked a piano. Piano, sewing machine—everything in the house.

"Yes, dear. The piano in our house came from Tennessee. That was Mildred's piano. And she played flute in high school. There's another little item for you."

"Piccolo."

"I beg your pardon?"

"She played piccolo. In the high school band."

My father refolded his handkerchief. "There's a horrible little side story about her clippings, by the way."

"What's that?"

He tipped to the side and put the handkerchief in a back pocket of his jeans. "Well, she and Leonard never got along. I would say they cordially hated each other. Leonard hated her because he was jealous that there was somebody else in my life and in my affections. And Mildred . . . Mildred was really very sweet. But she didn't like Leonard."

I thought about all the time she'd spent cooking the holiday meals Leonard and his family shared with us.

"One Sunday," my father was saying, "Leonard came down to the office and threw out all of her files. Mildred came in on Monday morning and asked me where I'd put her clippings, and of course I didn't know what she meant. She was crying. So I went into Leonard's room and he pretended he didn't know what I was talking about. But I finally nailed him. He admitted what he'd done. He said, 'I was cleaning up the office and I thought we needed the space.'

"And Mildred went home right then. Just walked out. I didn't quite know what to do, so I went home, too. She said, 'I'm never going back down there. I hate your brother!' I said, 'What do you want me to do? Do you want me to walk out on Leonard? What's it gonna be—me and you, kid? Should we start up another agency?' She stayed home for two or three days, and finally I persuaded her to come back."

"What year was that?"

" 'Fifty-one or 'fifty-two."

"So you were married then."

"We were married."

I thought of her wedding picture in the *Kingsport Times-News*—the only picture from that day I'd ever seen. Given to me by one of her friends, only weeks ago.

"Tell me about getting married," I said. "About marrying my mom."

Birdsong. Traffic sounds. I had all the time in the world.

"This would be the summer of 1950," my father began. He'd just returned from Michigan, a business trip to mollify a client, but he'd lost the account anyway.

"General Bertrandias called," he said. "He wanted me to come back into the service. He had a fancy-pantsy offer—I'd be a major or a lieutenant colonel or some goddamn thing. The Korean War was coming along. And it was very tempting. I was kind of fed up with advertising, and I was very fed up with Leonard. And I'd just lost a big account.

"I talked it over with Mildred, and she said, 'Why don't you think about it some more?' Well, one day we were walking home from work, and the subject came up again, about my going back into the service, and Mildred said, 'What about the idea of getting married?' "

"*She* asked *you?*"

"That's right."

"That's surprising."

"I don't know what's surprising about it, dear."

"She was a Southern girl. It was the fifties."

"She brought up the idea," he said firmly. "The idea of marriage was not my idea."

"Okay."

"I knew I liked being around her. We enjoyed working together. But the added dimension and responsibility of marriage was not my idea. Being married—you know, I'd just been through the meat grinder with Betty."

"So you were walking home," I prompted.

"We were walking up State Street when she brought up the subject in a very offhand way."

"Her proposal."

"That's your word."

"The 'idea of marriage.' "

"I said, 'It's not a bad idea, but I don't want any children.' And she said, 'Why not?' She'd stopped right in the middle of the sidewalk. I said, 'Well, I'm getting a little old to change diapers.' I was thirty-seven years old, you know. She was only twenty-seven. And she said, 'Okay, so we won't have children. Now, are we going to get married or not?' "

This was a punchline. He delivered it with a laugh. I closed my notebook and clicked off the tape.

"I hope I haven't offended you, dear."

"You know what?" I said, standing. "I think I'm going to stretch my legs. It's a beautiful day. I think I'm going to—"

"How will you—"

"—cruise around—"

"—get home?"

Home? I was backing away from the bench, but now I stopped. "Where did she go in California?" I asked.

"I beg your pardon?"

"When she was dying. Where did she go?"

He stood stiffly, reached down to rub his knee. "I think we're finished for today."

"I need to know where she went."

"That's enough, dear."

"Where did she go?"

He slammed his hands on the picnic table. *"Why are you doing this to me?"* he yelled.

"To *you?*" I said. Then I got it. Why he'd blurted as we drove past our churches. What he was saying now. I turned and jogged through the grass, my shoulder bag tucked under my arm like a football. I heard him calling my name but I kept going.

S pook was watching me from the floor. I slid my chair back from the table and patted my lap. The cat jumped up and began kneading my legs, her front paws pushing and curling as her purr revved. "Milk-treading" the zoologist Desmond Morris called it, an instinct triggered in the first blind moments after birth. The rhythm of little paws on a mother cat's stomach stimulates milk flow.

Inching back to the breakfast table, I waited until Spook furled herself into a contented oval. Then I flipped on the Smith-Corona and typed "To Whom it May Concern." I checked my notes, making sure the address was correct.

Then on to the letter: "Please release to my daughter Pamela Marin copies of all records pertaining to her mother, Mildred Marin." I read the sentence aloud. Would that be enough? "My wife, Mildred Marin," I added, "died on March 12, 1973."

Below a space for his signature I typed my father's name and address, then rolled in a new page and typed the letter again.

I'd had to listen to a lot of Muzak this past hour as I was shuttled from voice to voice on the line to Michael Reese Hospital, where my mother's mastectomy was performed in 1968, and Northwestern Memorial, where she died in '73. One clerk asked if my mother had "expired." My father's voice piped up in my head—*That's your word, dear.*

Both hospitals wanted to know if I was "next of kin."

"I'm her daughter," I'd said.

"Is your father deceased?"

Trick question. If "yes" was a shortcut through red tape, I'd take it. But I didn't want to lose access with a lie.

And wasn't I next of kin anyway? He just married her. I was blood.

"He lives," I'd said, and as I'd suspected, I needed his permission to get her files.

I was folding the letters into typed envelopes when the phone rang. I let the machine answer, running to the kitchen when I heard my name.

"Hi, I'm here."

"Oh. I see," my caller said. "Well, I have the information you were looking for."

I could picture her—a white-haired granny mouse with a whiskery chin mole. I'd spoken to her yesterday in the Christian Science Reading Room on Davis Street, where I'd gone as soon as the bus from Old Orchard brought me back to Evanston.

"Do you have a pen handy?" the granny mouse asked now.

"Yes." And I began taking notes as she spoke.

It was just as she'd thought, she said. There *was* a Christian Science retreat in California. In San Francisco. *Arden Wood,* I wrote. And its phone number. And the names of its chief administrator and nursing manager.

"I called the Mother Church," she said, using the term Christian Scientists use for the First Church in Boston, founded by Mary Baker Eddy shortly after she published her mind-over-matter tract, *Science and Health,* in 1875. My father had kept a copy of *Science and Health* on the nightstand by his side of the bed in Evanston. I knew that in his church that book was the basis for each Sunday's "lesson." Where we had a preacher who delivered a weekly sermon, they had two "readers" who stood onstage. One would read a Bible passage, then the other would read Mary Baker Eddy's interpretation of the passage in *Science and Health.* They took turns. Some of the congregants followed along in the books on their laps.

Mother Eddy, they called her.

Founder of the *Mother Church.*

"The lady I spoke with knew someone who'd been to Arden Wood," the granny mouse on the phone was saying. "She said it was just *gorgeous.*"

I thanked her and went outside for a smoke. Back in the kitchen I dialed the number in my notes.

"Good morning, this is Arden Wood." The voice almost a whisper.

"I'm calling for some information about someone who stayed there a while ago. Quite a while ago, actually. Nineteen seventy-three."

"I'm sorry, we only keep files for seven years. May I ask your name?"

I gave her my name and my address in Newport Beach, so she could send a brochure, then asked to speak with the chief administrator.

"He's not here today."

I asked for the nursing manager.

"I'm sorry, he's not here, either."

"Maybe you can tell me a little bit about the nursing program," I said. "I guess we're not talking about medical nurses."

"We don't use drugs or appliances, if that's what you're asking."

"So what do the nurses do?"

"Our nurses have been trained in a three-year program of Christian Science nursing."

"And what is that, exactly?"

"Well, bedside nursing," she said. "Feeding, washing, cleaning. Commoding. Mobility."

I couldn't speak. She whispered, "It's the kind of care, Pamela, that you would give that person at home."

* * *

I caught an Evanston Express train at the Main Street station and took it two stops to Howard Street, the end of the line. A city-bound el was disgorging rush-hour commuters as I crossed the platform. I got a window seat and watched the familiar stops tick by as the train rolled south. Bryn Mawr, Berwyn, Argyle. Belmont, Diversey, Fullerton.

The train dived underground at Division Street and I got out at the next stop, Chicago and State.

Crossing Rush, I glanced at the service door to the first kitchen I ever worked as a waitress—the Water Tower Hyatt's. I passed the old limestone Water Tower and the brown marble arch of Neiman Marcus, continuing along the Mercantile Mile to Ontario Street. And then I got my first jolt on today's ghost walk. Look at that. How many times had I seen it and not seen it? There was his building—Judy's building—his home. And there were the tan stone slabs of Northwestern Memorial Hospital. Where my mom died. One block away.

The doorman nodded as I entered. When I told him the apartment I'd come to visit he picked up his intercom.

"And who should I say you are?" he asked.

He was right to make me account for myself, I thought, as he murmured into his phone. He was right to give me the once-over as I waited to be buzzed through the security doors. I was a stranger here.

My father's girlfriend was waiting for me at her door.

"Hi Judy," I said, heading down sound-muffling carpet in the warm light of low-watt sconces.

"Your father's resting, Pamela," Judy said. She was still in her work clothes, a linen dress and stockings. A silky hidden layer hissed as she shifted her weight. Making no move to let me through the door.

"I just need a couple signatures," I said, producing my letters.

She read the addresses on the envelopes. I looked at my mother's wedding bands, the five rings Allan Marin had given

Mildred Lady in the First Baptist Church of Kingsport, Tennessee. The center band encircled with diamonds, bracketed by bands of rubies and sapphires, bookended with gold.

When had he put them on Judy's finger? How long had I seen them and not seen them there?

Her blue gaze was on me. "Your father was very upset when he got home yesterday," she said.

We were about the same height, though she must have weighed twice what I did. I leaned on the wall. "I'll stay here while you get those signatures."

Michael Reese Hospital is a cluster of smudge-colored buildings south of the Loop, halfway between the postcard skyline familiar to tourists and the gothic towers of the University of Chicago. I took a cab to the hospital's Blum Pavilion to meet the surgeon who'd performed my mother's mastectomy. I'd gotten his name from her medical file and arranged an interview, though once I was en route, speeding south on Lake Shore Drive, passing the flat black box of McCormick Place, I wondered what I wanted from Dr. Richard Bendix.

I was in the dreary lobby, looking through the photocopied microfiche given to me by the hospital's records department the day before, when I noticed an elegant older man stride from the sliding glass doors with an air of propriety that announced his status. Tall and angular, dressed in a well-cut dark suit, Bendix came straight to me, a thick lock of white hair dropping onto his forehead as we shook hands.

"Let me find us somewhere quiet to talk," he said, swiping at his forelock as he set off again. When he returned, his jacket replaced with a lab coat, he led me to a conference room.

Without preamble we established how my mother would have become his patient twenty years earlier—her gynecologist would have recommended an internist, who would have referred a surgeon. I knew the other doctors' names from her file. I'd tried to reach them, too, but they'd retired.

"I would have examined her, and have found she had a breast lump, and asked her to come in for a biopsy," Bendix said, his words suggesting that he didn't remember the patient. But why would he?

I asked about some handwritten notes in the file, and as he explained he took my pen and made a sketch that looked like an elephant with its trunk stuck in a mound of mashed potatoes—my mother's insides. Two swooping strokes signified the cuts he'd made. I couldn't follow his surgical descriptions. I wasn't really trying. It was a mistake, I realized, to have arranged a tutorial.

But on we went: A sample would have been taken from the lump, he said. Within minutes of its removal, Pathology would have reported to Surgery that the biopsy showed "infiltrating carcinoma"—her cancer had spread from breast to lymph nodes.

"At that time, in 'sixty-eight, radical mastectomy was the treatment," he said. A few days later he opened her up again and scooped out her ovaries, ridding her body of the estrogen that could accelerate cancer-cell growth.

I mentioned the hysterectomy she'd had six years earlier—a fact I'd just learned from her file.

"But she still had her ovaries," he said, "and the oncologist probably said that the best treatment was to remove them."

"What sort of follow-up treatment would have been recommended?"

"Well, she only had one node involved," he said, surprising me with his recall. But of course he would have reviewed her file, too. "At that time, with only one node involved, they felt that radiation would do more harm than good."

"They?"

"Radiation oncologists."

"And there wasn't chemo yet."

"No," he said, pushing the renegade forelock off his brow. "Not yet."

Ten minutes since I'd pressed *record,* and I was out of questions. And having a hard time meeting his steady gaze.

"May I ask," Bendix said, gently, "why after twenty years . . .?" He left his sentence hanging open.

My throat constricted. "I guess I didn't know too much about it back then," I said, busying myself with cassette and notebook. Then we were standing and I was thanking him, a horrible frozen expression I was trying to pass off as a smile making my face ache.

Back in a cab, I looked at Bendix's sketch. He'd drawn on the manila envelope that held my mother's records from Michael Reese. I returned it to my bag and took out her records from Northwestern Memorial Hospital. I hadn't broken the seal yet. What was I waiting for?

Unlike the blurry copies from Michael Reese's microfiche, Northwestern's file was on stark white paper with inch-thick borders of fresh-ink-cartridge black: The clerk sent to copy the file had left the copier's cover up, letting in peripheral light that made each page look like a newspaper ad *in memoriam.*

The top sheet was stamped EXPIRED. Below were intake forms, signed by my father. There were pages titled "Patient Progress Notes" filled with the script of various anonymous hands. "White female admitted from ER, very pale," from the night of March 11. "Feeling faint + generalized discomfort" the following afternoon.

My mother's attending physician, I discovered, was "Dr. J. Hines." The Hines family had lived in the house across the alley from ours, their fenced backyard visible in bare-limbed winter from my grandmother's rooms. We would sit in Nellie's Diner watching squirrels traverse phone lines as the Hines children played on their swing set below. The eldest son, James, had been my classmate at Lincoln Elementary.

I turned to my mother's "Medical Certificate of Death." The typed account reviewed her arrival in the ER, accompanied by her husband and Dr. Hines, wheeled in and immediately given blood, given oxygen, shot with needles bringing last-ditch hope.

Later, she was seen "thrashing about in bed," her "respiration labored."

Later, a doctor arrived to find "no resp, no pulse." It was 8:10 P.M., March 12, 1973.

A FedEx letter leaning on the Rosenbergs' front door: From Kevin. I sat on the concrete steps, in the shade of the pines, and opened it. He'd sent the new García Márquez. On the flyleaf of *Love in the Time of Cholera* he'd written "2PM, My love in the time of intolera-bly missing you."

Stuck in the book was a thick envelope from Dorothy. Not a letter, I saw, removing the pages inside, but copies from a Dobyns-Bennett High School reunion. Class of '41—my mother's. Dated 1969.

Their twenty-eighth?

I hurried through the alphabet to Mildred Lady Marin's entry:

> *Trained for four years at Harris School of Advertising Art in Nashville, then went North to Chicago seeking fame and fortune. Worked as an artist in an ad agency, a studio, and finally as a free-lance artist before becoming Art Director of ALLAN MARIN AND ASSOCIATES. I married the boss in 1950 and continued my career for a while.*
>
> *We now have two children: Richard Allan, a sturdy 12 year old who lives for auto-racing and trap-shooting, and Pamela Margaret, our slender 10 year old whose life centers on horses.*
>
> *We now live in Evanston—a quiet suburb with good schools, yards, etc., and Allan is active in civic affairs. I do volunteer work in our newly integrated school lunch program. In addition, I'm learning French and horseback riding. We have been able to travel a bit in recent years, also. Altogether, I've been very lucky and I hope all of you are having as much fun as we are!*

M y father was standing at his apartment door when I got off the elevator.

"Hey," I said.

"Hay is for horses," he said. When I reached him, he handed me a manila envelope.

"What's this?"

"My chapter about Mildred," he said, and stepped back to hold the door for me.

The entrance hall led past a galley kitchen and into the main room. When my father moved into Judy's one-bedroom a decade ago, they had a prime lake view. Now a row of high-rises filled the wraparound windows.

"Can I get you something to drink?" he asked. "Juice? Tea?"

"I'm fine," I said, dropping into a cane-backed chair at the wooden table from our dining room in Evanston. I wondered if this chair was the one we'd parked near the kitchen door between meals—the one I pushed to my place at the table for family dinners and Sunday lunch. The table's octagonal base sprouted a trunk that widened at the top to support a round tabletop. I remembered how the terraced octagon felt under bare feet.

My father brought glasses of ice water from the kitchen and sat in one of the two chairs in the dining set that had arms. His or my mom's, it would have been. His now. He pushed aside a cup of black Flair pens, day planner, letter opener, phone. His office supplies were guarded by a six-inch silver knight on horseback who had ridden the desk at his agency.

He reached out and tapped the envelope he'd given me. "I think you'll find what you're looking for in here."

The knight's helmet was the size of a thimble. Inside was a finely carved ivory head. His lance slid from an armored glove and his feet could be pulled from the tiny stirrups. I remembered playing with him. I turned on my cassette recorder. "So we got to 1950 the last time," I said.

He took a sip of water.

"You two were about to get married," I said.

My father looked at the windows. He was dressed as he had been on summer weekends in Evanston—tan linen slacks, open-collar dress shirt, polished loafers. I noticed a dash of shaving cream by his ear.

"Well," he said, finally, "Nellie had come to Chicago, and interviewed me at lunch."

He described my grandmother as "a sweet, smiley Southern lady" who "never asked a straightforward question." She "secured her information indirectly," he said. Regarding her twenty-seven-year-old daughter's decision to marry, Nellie asked the thirty-seven-year-old suitor, "Did you enjoy your previous marriage?"

"That's a good line," I said, wondering if it appeared on a page in the manila envelope. I asked about Henry.

"Mildred had given me a sketchy outline of the rise and fall of Henry Lady before I went down there," he said. "She referred to him as a very plain man. She said, 'You might not understand him.' "

"Why would she think that?"

"Because I'm a city boy, Pamela. And Henry was . . . I don't mean this in a derogatory sense, but I thought he was a nice hick."

"Did the families get along?"

"I don't understand your question."

"At the wedding. And after." I was trying to imagine my dark-eyed, sleekly groomed Grandfather Marin—the dapper gent in the studio portrait that had hung in our house—sitting in a pew with the Baptists on Church Circle.

"Mother wouldn't go to Kingsport," he said. "She copped out by saying Dad couldn't stand the trip. Mother was very devious."

"Was Jacob sick?"

"Well, he was not in great health, but that's another subject. I don't think Mother wanted to be there."

He'd never talked much about his mother, Gertrude Marin. I had a few snapshot memories of an old lady dressed in black in a stuffy room. Was it a nursing home room? With a big red Oriental rug. I must have been down on the rug while the grownups talked.

"Why didn't your mother want to go to your wedding?" I asked.

"I don't know, dear. You're asking me to describe another person's state of mind."

"What about Lois and Leonard?" I said, naming his sister and brother.

"The only person I had was Leonard."

"Lois didn't go?"

"No."

"Any friends from Chicago?"

"No."

We moved on: Florida honeymoon. Mildred moves into Allan's apartment on Astor Street, in the northside's tony Gold Coast neighborhood. Long walks on Michigan Avenue to and from Allan Marin & Associates. Late-night jam sessions on ad campaigns. I let him fill one side of a cassette tape describing the townhouse on nearby Elm Street that they bought from warring siblings and renovated on weekends. I tried to picture them knocking down walls and sanding floors, dust-covered, side by side, while he told me in surprising detail about loans they'd taken out, construction costs, the personalities of workmen hired to help out and neighbors they came to know.

"We moved in on Mildred's birthday," he was saying, as I flipped over the tape. I pressed *record*.

"February 22, 1953," he said.

Her thirtieth.

The Wise Man who'd stood on a pedestal behind our piano was over by the windows. The large oil painting of a woman in blue that had hung over the blue couch in our living room filled a wall here. On the carpet, used as a doorstop, was a chipped ceramic pitcher. It had sat in a matching bowl on my grandmother's dresser.

"When did you change your mind about having kids?" I asked.

"I don't recall."

"There must have been some discussion."

"I don't recall any."

"Try."

He crossed his arms over his chest. I had all the time in the world.

"I was ambivalent about having children," he said. "I neither wanted them nor unwanted them. It wasn't a big thing for me. But it became obvious to me that for the long run, Mildred was not going to be happy at the agency."

"Why was that?"

"I just thought it, dear," he said. "That's just how I felt."

"Okay."

"And we began trying to have a child, and we tried for about a year—unsuccessfully. And I remember one day I picked her up at her doctor's office and she was crying. And we went home, and I tried to comfort her. I said, 'Listen, I think we're going about this the wrong way. I'm not a doctor, and I don't know anything about blowing out tubes and all that other medical bullshit he's been giving you. But I think that you're under too much stress at the agency.' "

So she quit, and stayed at home on Elm Street, and got pregnant.

Medical bullshit.

I prompted him through tales of my brother's babyhood, reminding myself to be a reporter, to stay with the rhythm, ask a question, listen, follow up.

Frankie came to clean the Elm Street apartment twice a week. My parents and brother took nightly strolls through Lincoln Park. Nellie visited from Tennessee. I pictured the house in Kingsport that Nellie's mother bought for Henry and Nellie after Henry's bankruptcy, one of the Tudors in Dorothy's neighborhood. My mother had gone back to that house to tend her dying father when she was pregnant with me.

"Tell me about Nellie coming to live with us," I said.

"She came up in, let's see, the fall of 'fifty-eight."

"After Henry died."

"That's right. Mildred had been running back and forth to Kingsport, and I finally said, 'This is bullshit. Nellie should come up here and have the apartment on the first floor.' Well, Nellie's reaction to that was terrible at first. You know, 'I'm from the South, and all my friends are here . . .' And I said, 'Mildred can't keep racing to Tennessee every twenty minutes. She's got a child! She needs to be at home.' "

The memory brought color to his face. He took a sip of water to calm down. Then he laughed.

"I got Nellie—God, it was really very funny—I got Nellie to come up on the basis that she'd bring some of her stuff to Chicago, and leave the rest in Kingsport. 'If you change your mind, you can always move back'—that was my pitch. Hang on to the house—rent it—and come on up. And she thought that was a good idea. Her entire life had been down in that little town. And I felt I couldn't sell her on a clean break. Of course, once we got to Evanston, she was really quite thrilled."

"Why?"

"Well, dear, a house like that, with four Corinthian columns— that was a bit of all right."

We were up to 1960. He grew animated again, describing how he'd financed the house, and the work assigned to contractors hired to reconfigure the second floor to include an apartment for my grandmother that was about the size of the one we were sitting in now. I let him talk. I put in a new tape. Then I mentioned my mother's hysterectomy.

"I guess she had it in 1962," I said.

"That's news to me."

"You didn't know she had a hysterectomy?"

"I know she had one, dear, but that date isn't fixed in my mind."

"She was pretty young—thirty-nine. Do you remember what was happening with her physically?"

"I don't recall."

"Anything she said about it? Conversations you had?"

"Did that turn up on the medical records?"

"Yes."

"I have a complete blank on that."

"I thought you said you remembered—"

"I *know* that there was *this experience,* but the experience is a blank in my mind. How far along are we on your grocery list?"

"When did she tell you she had a lump in her breast?"

"What are you talking about?"

"Her left breast. The one they cut off."

He waved the question away. "That's in my chapter about Mildred."

"I haven't read your chapter."

"Well, why don't we resume after you have? Shall we?"

"She went to Michael Reese on May 5, 1968," I said. "She was in the hospital for seventeen days."

"Are you asking me a question?"

"Did you take me to visit her?"

"I took Nellie. I don't recall taking the children."

"I was nine. What was I told?"

He plucked a Flair pen from the cup in front of him, tapped it on the table, flipped it over, tapped the other end. He did that with silverware in restaurants when he didn't like the service. "You were told that your mother was in the hospital," he said. "As I recall, the decision was made not to go into any details."

"The decision made by both of you."

"Yes, dear, obviously. It had to be our mutual wish, or how could I pull it off? She could have told you."

"Good point. She had two operations—"

"That's in the chapter."

"The first operation—"

"As I wrote in my chapter," he said, his voice rising, "she had an operation to remove malignant tissue, which involved her left breast, and under her left arm. And they were ready to release her and then they took another picture, more pictures, and they decided to go back in again."

"Were other doctors consulted?"

Tap-tap, flip, tap-tap. "No."

"Wouldn't it have been—"

"They consulted with *me!*" he yelled. And I had to fight the urge to get up and strike him. Back of my hand to the side of his head. I could see myself doing it.

Instead, I asked a question. "Do you remember her doctors' names?"

"No."

"What sort of follow-up treatment did she have?"

"I don't recall."

"Did she ever see a doctor again, after she left the hospital?"

"I was not aware of any medical supervision after that point."

"Whose idea was California?"

"What?"

"Arden Wood," I said.

"The rest home?"

"Yes."

"Is that the name of it?"

"Yes."

He glared at me. "Your mother became interested in Christian Science with no prodding or selling on my part."

"Really?"

"*Never!*" he said, throwing down the pen.

"Okay."

"She became interested in Science in the early seventies because she saw how it was working for me."

"How so?"

"You're being very pressy, Pamela."

"How was Christian Science working for you?"

"Various physical problems. And your mother became interested, and all of a sudden she started appearing in church."

"In *your* church?"

"Yes, dear."

"Where was I?"

"Well, I guess she parked you at the Sunday school next door."

"She stopped going to the Baptist church?"

"Intermittently," he said. "She came to our service intermittently, as she became interested in Science. And I got her a copy of *Science and Health.* And then she wanted to go see a practitioner." He picked up the pen and put it back in the cup. "I think she was preparing herself to attempt to work out her problem in Science."

"What 'problem'?"

He looked to the windows. "The general expression of physical complaint was referred to as a 'backache.' That's what she termed it. 'My back feels stiff.' Or 'Sometimes I have difficulty walking because my back is bothering me.' And I referred her to a practitioner."

No prodding or selling on my part.

I said, "She told the Christian Science practitioner she had backache?"

"The discussion between a practitioner and a patient is confidential. I don't know what she told her practitioners."

" 'Practitioners'? She had more than one?"

"There was one in Evanston, one in Wilmette. There was a married couple, both practitioners, in Arlington Heights. They moved to California."

"Is that why she went to California? To see them?"

Moments passed. I followed his gaze to the neighboring highrises. He spoke without turning from the view.

"Mildred fell down the stairs in December," he said. "But she insisted on going through the holiday routines. Christmas was a big thing for Mildred, all the decorations, the tree. She made a big thing out of Christmas, right to the very end.

"I waited until the festivities were behind us, and then I told her, 'I think the time has come for you to make a major decision. You either want to go the medical route, or the Christian Science route. And I'll back you up either way.' She said, 'I would like to go to a Christian Science rest home.' I said, 'Where'd you get that idea?' And she had all the details. 'There's Chestnut Hill, in Massachusetts,' she said. 'And there's so-and-so in California.' I said, 'Well, if that's what you want to do, I'll make the arrangements.' "

So-and-so in California.

"What was I told about the trip?"

"You were told that your mother was going on a vacation."

"How long was she gone?"

"Ten weeks," he said. "I wrote her three or four letters—no response. We got into February, and of course her birthday was coming, and I didn't know if she was coming back for her birthday. It would have been her fiftieth birthday. I was wondering, you know, are we going to pretend it isn't, or what?

"Well, I got her a present, but I didn't know whether to send it. I thought maybe if I sent her a birthday present that was going to give her the wrong signal. You know—Here you are, happy birthday, see you around. So I hung on to it.

"And she finally called me—I'm working backward from March 12. Let's see, she called me sometime between the fifth and tenth of March, and she said, 'I'm ready to come home.' And I said, 'Fine. When?' She wanted to come home on Saturday. I said, 'Fine, I'll meet you at the airport.' And she said, 'If you want to meet me with a wheelchair, that's fine.'

"Well, when she got back Saturday I was scared out of my wits. I brought her home, and I kept saying, 'I've got to get Dr. Hines in here.' She said no. I said, 'Well, you can't just be here. I mean, you obviously require some attention, and you obviously haven't gotten whatever you went to California to get.' " His voice was rising again, agitated. "I said, 'The only option now is medical procedure!' "

He pushed his chair back and stood up. I waved my hands. "Please," I said, pointing to the cassette. I was crying. "Please. Let's finish."

He picked up his glass and rattled the ice, drank till the water was gone. Then he sat. When he began again his voice was calm. "It was ten o'clock at night, Saturday night, and she sent me out for some Juicy Fruit chewing gum. That's what she wanted," he said. "She had a cough. I said, 'Do you want anything else?' Her color was practically gray. Her eyes were lusterless. And she had this *godawful* cough. She said, 'I just want some Juicy Fruit.'

"Well, we got through Saturday night, and Sunday morning I went to church. And I said, 'Now, listen. I'm really not going to listen to you anymore. I'm going to have Jim Hines come over here right after lunch today.' And he did. And Jim and I took her to the hospital on Sunday night. And she died the following morning, Monday morning."

"Wait. *Wait.* She died on Sunday night," I said. I came home from Laura's farm on Sunday night. The porch light was on, the house was dark, I ran inside—

"No she didn't, dear. She died on Monday. Actually, it wasn't

Monday morning, because I saw her Monday on my way down to the office."

"But she died Sunday night."

"Dear, your mother died on March 12. *Monday,* March 12."

"Where was I on Monday?"

"You were at school, Pamela. I stopped in to see her before I went to the office, and we had a very brief talk. I said, 'I'll see you on my way home.' And I stopped in again on my way home. Then I went right back down there with you. I would say it was about seven o'clock when we got there. And she had passed. So I would say she probably passed away between five and seven o'clock."

"It was later," I said, wiping my eyes.

"I beg your pardon?"

"It was eight-ten."

Coast Highway is the scenic route from Newport Beach to San Francisco, a 450-mile stop-and-go through beach towns and barren shoreline. Interstate 5 cuts a businesslike stripe through an inland valley. I hadn't decided which road to take when I climbed into my car before dawn with a thermos of coffee, map, notebook and a change of clothes. I warmed the engine and studied the map. As I pulled away I noticed that my landlord's girlfriend had left her windows open again.

I took the 55 freeway to the I-5, which led me past the Band-Aid-colored offices of the *Orange County Register* in Santa Ana, past Disneyland's Matterhorn in Anaheim. I was front-running the weekday rush into L.A. Since it didn't matter which road I traveled, I'd chosen the truck-jammed dragstrip that would get me north quicker.

I had completed and returned a "Special Application For Our Non-Science Friends" that was mailed to me by the whispering woman who'd answered the phone at Arden Wood when I called from the Rosenbergs' kitchen.

"With what church, religious organization or ethical society have you been associated during the past five years?" the application queried. Trick question? I answered with plain truth: *None.* Notice of my confirmed reservation arrived with a form letter from the chief administrator addressed "To Our Very Special Rest and Study Guest." Above an inked signature, the administrator closed his note "Lovingly."

It didn't matter which road I traveled. She'd flown. Then taken a cab, probably. Arden Wood, not far from Golden Gate

Park, close to the sea, looked to be a shuttle-precluding distance from the airport. But I didn't want to think about that section of the map yet. And I didn't want to fill my droning Tercel with radio's advisers and quipsters and jingled pitches. Or its music: I hadn't been able to listen to music for months. Music cut too deep. It reached in and mucked about. Now of all times I wanted to keep the focus outbound. I needed to be an observer, a fact finder. I had to get through this.

In darkness I threaded the scrub hills north of L.A., passed the Tinkertoy structures of an amusement park, fought the undertow of big rigs rolling on paired tires taller than my car. Two hours from home, the new day alight, I watched a muscle truck haul a slatted trailer onto the freeway. An arm tattooed shoulder to wrist rested on the driver's door. In back, its black tail swirling, was a brown horse with blinders over its eyes—leather pieces shaped like cupped hands. Horses have a wide span of peripheral vision, and can be frightened by motion on either flank. Sometimes horse handlers use blinders to block out all but what's directly ahead—to calm a nervous animal, or to help a work horse focus on a task. I pulled even with the trailer, stealing glances at the swaybacked bay rocking with the rhythm of the road. When it turned its head, I saw that the leather cups affixed to the old bay's halter covered its eyes completely. It was riding blind, a hostage. What would be spookier than that?

The hills grew and backed off the road. Now the valley was a tan-and-green quilt pinned together with phone poles and metal towers, laced with cables and wire. I passed vineyards and or-chards and tilled soil ready to plant, passed through the shit-stink of a slaughter yard filled with cattle and then through acres of spidery windmills cranking electricity from thin air. I pulled off once to fill the tank, my stomach lurching in the fumes. And then I was in the outer fringe of San Francisco, I was almost there, and I had to pay attention to road signs leading me from this freeway to that, taking me west, north, west again, over the bay on the Oakland Bridge and onto streets lined with houses that looked like they were made of marzipan.

From this street to that. I knew their names from the map. The neighborhood I'd circled in my dark car seven hours earlier had a numeric grid bisecting an alphabetized grid. Fifteenth Avenue took me across Santiago, Taraval, Ulloa, Vicente. Next would be Wawona. I'd mailed my application to Arden Wood Benevolent Association, 445 Wawona.

I crossed Vicente and pulled to the curb. Fifteenth dead-ended one block down—a forty-five-degree angle downhill—at a wall of eucalyptus trees, green-black under a white sky. I'd read about those trees. A *grove,* it said in the brochure sent to me with my reservation. Twelve acres, it said. I could picture what I couldn't see: The terraced paths at the base of the trees. Leafy gardens of deep-shade thrivers. And the massive structure at the grove's core, castlelike, institutional, with four or five wings, five or six tan stucco stories up to a sharply pitched tile roof.

Benevolent Association.

My mother had been here, too. A *rest and study guest,* welcomed *lovingly.* And when her cabbie crested Vicente and sped down to Wawona, hurtling toward that curved driveway leading into the green-black grove, she would have felt gravity strong-arming her, shoving her against the vinyl seat, pinning her—

I couldn't do it.

I killed the engine and crawled into the backseat and wept, and then I fell asleep. When I woke the sky was gritty. I knew what I had to do.

Up the driveway, park. This kind of entrance is called a portecochère. Automatic doors: for the weak and weary, for cane users and the wheelchair-bound. High ceilings and muted upholstery on armchairs and couches with spindly curved legs. That furniture style is called Queen Anne.

Another granny mouse at the desk, with dandruff, smiling, credit card, room key. Dinner service has started, she says. It's 4:30.

I take the stairs up. In my room a pink rose on an empty desk, two armchairs by a floor lamp, narrow bed in the corner. I go to the window. The eucalyptus trees are rooted on a slope. Ten stories tall, they must be. Leaves shaped like scythes, bark sloughed in sheets.

What's this by the door—an intercom?

Radio. I turn the knob. A hymn played on an organ, voiceless. On another channel a woman reads—a Reader, I can tell, by the tortured language. These are Mary Baker Eddy's words, probably from *Science and Health:*

"Mind is not the author of matter, and the creator of ideas is not the creator of illusions. Either there is no omnipotence, or omnipotence is the only power. God is the infinite, and infinity never began, will never end, and includes nothing unlike God . . ."

I take the stairs down to the dining room and wade in among cloth-draped fourtops bathed in soft light, aware of a dozen gray heads turning to follow my progress, aware of the watery gazes on me, the frank appraisals. I go to a table in a corner. I can't look at the elderly waitress when I order. I don't wait for the food. I'm off before she returns, back in the stairwell, up to my room.

My mother fell on the stairs in December.

She had a backache, she said.

She told her husband she wanted to come here and he bought her a plane ticket, gave her money, drove her to the airport.

White tile in the bathroom. Hot water thundering into the tub. I lower myself inch by inch, a blood-rush scalding. Steam clouds the view.

Steam clouds, water blurs, but look: They said five years, then we'll know. They said five years when they did this—cutting, excavating, stitching. Look what they did. Here's what's left. It's January 1973. Four and a half years have passed. She closes her eyes.

We shall not cease from exploration
And the end of all our exploring
Will be to arrive where we started
And know the place for the first time.

T. S. Eliot
"Little Gidding"
Four Quartets

Part Three

Home

S mile," Kevin said. We were on the beach, taking turns posing with our infant son. It was August 1993. Cal was one month old that day. In two weeks I would be thirty-five.

Bare feet cooling in the Pacific, my boy burrito bundled in my arms, I beamed at the camera. Kevin had already captured my new-minted joy in dozens of photos since Cal's birth. We both noticed that my expression had altered in some fundamental way. Motherhood had given me a smile that was wide open, as my body had been, withholding nothing.

"Your turn," I said, handing Cal to his dad.

The stretch of water and sky we were using as a backdrop was in Huntington Beach, a few blocks from our home. Three years earlier we'd moved from the rented half-a-shack in nearby Newport Beach, where we'd displaced a forest of pot plants with our futon, to a bungalow of our own. The house we bought looked like the ones little kids draw—a box topped with an upside-down V roof, the front door bracketed by windows. Before we had a baby we'd babied our property, weeding and seeding and planting magnolia trees out front, sinking an Australian willow and a eucalyptus sapling into the sandy soil of our small back-yard. The eucalyptus had silvery leaves the color of the stucco the seller had larded onto his termite-riddled investment.

We settled into homemaking, and another kind of settling began. When I had returned from Arden Wood, in the summer of 'eighty-eight, I curled up on the futon in our bedroom-greenhouse and stayed there for weeks. The boxes I'd shipped from Kingsport and Chicago, and the treasures too precious to part with, which I'd hauled home in carry-on bags, were stacked against the unpainted wallboard at the back of the closet. I threw a sheet over my keepsakes, pulled another up to my chin. Too many tapes were playing and rewinding in my head. I silenced the chorus with dreamless sleep.

I got out of bed to spend my thirtieth birthday on Catalina Island. Kevin had planned the trip right down to heart-shaped balloons in our hotel room. The day my mother turned thirty, she and my forty-year-old father moved into a townhouse on Elm Street that they'd bought from warring siblings and renovated on weekends. They used hours not devoted to their work—ad campaigns and marketing schemes for clients of Allan Marin & Associates—to make a home for themselves in a ritzy neighborhood off the northern tip of Michigan Avenue known as the Gold Coast. I thought about my still-young not-yet-mother at thirty, a commercial artist in what might have been the most hope-filled and engaging period of her life, as I ate ceviche and drank margaritas and walked a strand across a blue channel from the shrouded boxes in my closet.

Slowly, as seasonless months emptied into one another, I picked up the rhythms of my life as it was before I went to Tennessee.

Kevin and I rose early to read the papers in a window booth at Charlie's Chili, watching surfers ride the break at Newport Pier. I dusted off my dressed-up journo duds and went back out on the soc beat for Ann Conway, the *Los Angeles Times*'s society columnist in Orange County. As before, freelancing for Ann brought me other assignments from the *Times*.

Between deadlines I wrote a novel about two sisters whose mother had died of breast cancer when they were teens. Growing up in "a college town north of Chicago," the girls attended Sunday services at a Baptist church with their mom, a former commercial artist, while their adman dad worshiped with Christian Scientists in the church next door. Woven with the thin plot, set when the sisters were in their twenties, were scenes from their Tennessee-born mother's life, including her last days in a hotel room in Northern California.

The older sister was a quick-tempered painter named Pamela who'd moved to a suburb south of L.A. The younger sister, a lonely waitress in Chicago, got my middle name, Margaret. The dead mom was Elizabeth—my mother's middle name. *Since She Went Away* I called it. An agent sent copies to publishers, forwarding their rejection letters to my new home in Huntington Beach. Even before the agent and I decided to call it quits I recognized my roman à clef as something other than fiction. Writing it, I suspected, had been therapy. I'd taken the typing cure.

I shelved the manuscript and turned to my research. For all the painstaking effort that went into gathering the facts and artifacts of my mother's life, I'd abandoned the project when I got home. I knew and didn't want to know what was in those boxes and carry-on bags. As time passed, a sense of dread attached to them. I was afraid that opening them would trigger the enervating sadness of my long day's journey to Arden Wood.

But I wasn't done trying to understand my mother, much as I wished that I were. I had failed to conjure her in fiction. Now it was time to finish what I'd started as a reporter.

As with my search, I began with Tennessee. I'd collected more than a hundred photos there, including studio portraits of my ancestors posing near the dawn of popular photography, when the Eastman Kodak plant in Kingsport, belching black smoke and spewing chemicals into the Holston River, had first drawn hard-scrabbling farmers into town for the relatively easier life of factory work. I made an album with typed photo captions. "Nashville, 1943. Advertising Art School students outside studio." "June, 1947. Newport Beach, California." Then I dug into my files—the transcripts, public records, scrapbook pages and weathered newsprint I'd studied in Dorothy's guest bedroom with my back to the pastel portrait of a blue-eyed boy my mother gave her best friend *in memoriam*. I reread it all, cleared a file drawer of my clips and writer's miscellany, and stored Act One of Mel's life chronologically.

On to Chicago, and the heavy lifting.

After my father had recounted his last days with my mom— recording, dry-eyed, his dry account of her homecoming—I saw him once more before I left town. In one of our taped talks he mentioned a storage locker that contained furnishings from Evanston. That was news. When I looked up the address of the warehouse he named, I discovered that it was only blocks from the bars where I'd waitressed a decade earlier: If the room I'd rented when I worked at the 2350 Pub had been up a few more flights of rubber-lined stairs, I could have seen the warehouse from my makeshift desk as I learned to type. How about that. I was floundering out of my teens and into my twenties—moving from one crap job to another, one unloved apartment to the next—while my bankrupt father, ensconced in his girlfriend's high-rise, kept bits and pieces from Forest Avenue close at hand. That I might have wanted to share the loot was just another fatherly notion that never occurred to my father.

I'd focused on the furniture as I finished my research in Chicago. Thinking about furniture helped block out the crushing new awareness that one lost day fifteen years earlier, when I was fourteen and my mother had just turned fifty, I was only a few miles from her as she suffered through her final hours.

It was a half-hour cab ride from our house to the hospital.

Twice that would have gotten me there on the el.

Between breakfast and lunch I could have walked to her. Why hadn't I?

What kind of family goes about its business—off to church, to school, to work—while one member languishes in a hospital bed?

What kind of family lets a mother die alone?

I called the warehouse and learned two things: First, my father's storage space was in his name and his girlfriend's, and I couldn't get in without one of them. Also, their bill was in arrears.

"How much do they owe?" I asked.

The clerk cleared her throat. "We've been trying to reach them."

"Three months?"

"Um . . ."

"Six?"

"Excuse me." She put me on hold. When she returned she said, "I really can't discuss this account with you, Mrs. Marin."

"My mother was 'Mrs. Marin,' " I said. "There *is* no *Mrs. Marin*—that's the problem."

"I'm sorry."

I should have been the one apologizing but I had another question. "What happens if they don't pay their bill?"

"The contents go to auction."

And maybe that's what my father and his girlfriend had wanted. Maybe they wanted the remnants of his life with a wife and children to simply disappear. My father had already done an edit on the estate, taking our dining room table, the carved Wise Man and other choice pieces with him to his high-rise hideout. He'd given his girlfriend all of my mother's jewelry, all her silver, her china and glassware, the lace tablecloth my grandmother had made with a reed-thin crochet needle bobbing through loops of silky white thread.

Nesting with his prized possessions, he'd left the rest to rot. And now here I'd come, stumbling down memory lane, and tripped on his trove. I squawked about the bill. They paid. A few days later we met at the warehouse.

Two bulky workmen took us up in a freight elevator and unlocked a storage unit about the size of Helluva Note's stall at Peebles' Stables. At my direction, they began unpacking the space. Furniture that had decorated my dreams emerged from the deep darkness of the storage box into the semidarkness of the dusty hallway piece by piece: The barrel-shaped nightstands from my parents' turquoise bedroom. A wing chair with floral upholstery my mother had embroidered in bright shades of yarn. The orange chaise she'd slouched in as she read detective novels, each paperback cover illustrated with a busty woman in peril, cowering.

I watched in stunned silence until my father picked up a small cardboard box, saying it held photos he wanted to give to my brother. His words hit me like poisoned darts. I leapt at him, arms flailing, the fury I'd choked back for weeks streaming from me—

*"What the fuck are you doing? Why do you think I'm here, asshole? For the fucking lamps? Give me that box! Fucking give it to me **now**! And keep your goddamn hands off the rest of this . . ."*

The workmen backed into the shadows and lit cigarettes. I crowded my father away from the storage space, railing at him, my spit strafing his starched collar. He stepped into the elevator. One of the workers followed. I was still yelling as the metal doors clanged shut and my father descended—to hell for all I cared.

I dried my face on my shirttail, bummed a smoke from the other workman. When my anger ebbed I walked back down the twilit corridor to see what I could spirit away.

I wanted to take it all. "Pack it up, boys," I would have liked to say, dropping my address with the office clerk on my way out. Then I could have sorted the scraps of my inheritance at my leisure—at home. But I didn't have that luxury.

I couldn't afford the cross-country move, for starters, and didn't have room in my half-a-shack for the many large pieces that had filled our large house. And even if I'd had the money and the space, my father would have had to sign off on the shipment—not bloody likely now. He and his girlfriend were ready to let this lot go to auction. But give it to me? The answer to that unasked question sparkled on her ring finger. Back when I was a lonely waitress in Chicago, before I became a quick-tempered writer in a suburb south of L.A., my father had slipped onto his girlfriend's hand the five thin bands my mother had worn for twenty-two years.

That day in the warehouse I stacked my to-go pile with portable goods—books, papers, photographs. Reporter's tools. I worked quickly, knowing that at any moment my father or his girlfriend could have me booted. And I wept, a pitiful ghost in that cavernous dreamscape, as I would years later, unpacking my relics at home.

Here was my mother's high school yearbook, a *1941 Maroon and Grey*. In Kingsport, Virgie and John I. Cox had given me an anonymous copy from an earlier print run, along with their memories of my young grandparents and infant mom. But this yearbook had been my mother's—the only one bearing her signature, filled with hastily penned compliments and good-luck wishes from her friends.

Here was a thick brown leather-bound book, *World-Famous Paintings,* published in 1939 and probably bought that year, as my mom went off to art school in Nashville. On the tarnished flyleaf, in careful script: "To Mildred Lady . . . From Elliott." The former snack shop employee, who'd risen through the Eastman's ranks to retire as food-services manager, Elliott Armbrister had told me of his and my mother's youthful romance with greater tenderness than any of my father's memories.

I'd found a well-thumbed book of piano études, its pages pencil-marked by an exacting teacher, my mother's name and address on the cover in a childish hand. "Mildred Lady, 205 Compton Terrace"—the mock Tudor duplex Henry and Nellie had shared with Dorothy Hale's family, across the park from the house where I was Dorothy's guest. Henry had hocked the family piano, I'd learned in the Blountville courthouse. My father had told me the upright in our dining room in Evanston, backed by a custom-built pedestal for our Wise Man, came North with my mom.

I'd filled boxes with books on fine art, commercial art, gardening, sewing, religion—volumes from our library that would have been my mother's. And I'd found some of my grandmother's books in storage, too, including a tattered nineteenth-century work of inspirational writing called *Stepping Heavenward,* by a "Mrs. E. Prentiss," inscribed by a ten-year-old farm girl, "Nellie King White, Dec. 25, 1906."

Left to rot. Most likely headed for the auction block. As were the four artworks waiting in there for me.

Two of them, framed and well-preserved, were charcoal portraits on brown paper. Wiping the dusty glass with my shirttail, I'd recognized the stern-faced couple as my mother's paternal grandparents, William Melvin and Nettie Bruner Lady. Before my trip I hadn't known their names. By the time I got to Chicago I had photos of them and word pictures drawn by the last of their eight children, my great-aunt Mandy, who in her tenth decade was still wrestling with memories of her smooth-talking brother Henry bankrupting the family. By the time I got to Chicago I'd spent hours in the grass by William and Nettie's hilltop headstone, overlooking the churchyard my mom took me to when we stayed at the Farm.

The other two pieces were oil on canvas. I'd found them at the back of the storage space, tossed in an open carton on the concrete floor. In time-darkened pigment, layered with grime, each bore the pale outline of a face, the sweeping strokes of long dark hair. Though the facial features were nearly unreadable, I could tell they were self-portraits, and guessed that one was the picture my father had seen on the drawing board in my mother's garret when she was a single working artist in Chicago.

Here were my touchstones. I knew it when I first held them, in mote-filled semidarkness, racing a warehouse clock. As I peeled bubblewrap from them years later in Huntington Beach, the thought coursed through me again: This was as close as I would get. Whatever I learned, felt, dreamed, theorized about my mother—I'd have to measure my perceptions against these bits of brittle cloth and aged paint. Here was my mother looking at herself, revealed and transfigured by her own hand.

What had she seen?

I found out after taking the paintings to a conservator recommended by the L.A. County Museum of Art. When he'd completed a museum-quality restoration—the checklist attached to his bill filled a single-spaced page—my mother's self-portraits glistened with life. Under the grubby surface of those discarded canvases was work that suggested Mildred Lady's ambition had been matched by talent. One portrait was glamorous, the other plain. In both the artist rendered her sadness, her defiance, her strength. This was my mother, then and always, as I had already come to know her.

I hung the portraits by my desk, above the computer that had replaced my Smith-Corona. I looked at my mother and talked to her and imagined her watching me as I worked. By then I was pregnant. I bought a gold-tooled journal and taped my first ultrasound photo inside. Onto that starry midnight sky—my insides revealed and transfigured—the ultrasound technician had typed labels: "Uterus." "Gestational sac." "Baby." The dense little packet of multiplying cells that would become my son was the size and shape of a pistachio nut. "Dear Pistachio," I wrote, and filled the journal with what I thought a grown child might one day wonder about a mother.

When Cal was born I sent my father and his girlfriend a birth announcement. We'd been out of touch for years. Their response was silence.

No card, no call, not so much as a floppy sun hat for my boy?

"We don't want anything from them," Kevin said, and I could let that be right because I had him, and now we had Cal.

By the time Cal was toddling around the neighborhood, we'd filled a shelf with photo albums of our smiling threesome. One day a few weeks after Cal's second birthday, as I was taking snaps of him splashing in a wading pool in our front yard, a FedEx truck pulled up under the magnolias. I signed for the delivery and opened it absentmindedly, keeping watch over my son.

The package held a paperback, my father's self-published autobiography. *Allan in Wonderland* he'd called it. A photo of him filled the cover. By the look of his long sideburns I guessed the picture dated from the seventies. His eyes were shaded by his hat's wide brim. I tossed the book onto the porch without looking inside.

Was I cruel to write him out of my life? That was the opinion of his sister Lois, whom I'd been taken to visit at her home in Milwaukee maybe three times in my childhood. When I was eight months pregnant, Aunt Lois phoned from gilded retirement in Palm Beach to kvetch—I was callous, selfish, a horrible person for the way I treated her brother, my dad. Kevin had returned from errands to find his hormonally unbalanced supersized wife sobbing under the backyard willow. He called Lois back to suggest, politely, what she might do with her opinions.

My father was ill. At the end of my pregnancy and first weeks of maternity he'd been in the hospital for prostate surgery. During one marathon postpartum night, as I shuffled from bed to bathroom to glider, my underside torn and leaking, my breasts painfully engorged, nipples raw with blood blisters from first-time nursing—my brother called, as Lois had, to badger me. He yelled at me, threatened me, slammed down the receiver and redialed my number until I finally unplugged the phone.

My father was sick, but I didn't call him, I didn't send a card. In truth I didn't give him much thought at all. If that was selfish, so be it. I needed to get my strength back, to heal. And I was trying to figure out how to be a mom.

Cal was still playing in the wading pool that summer day as Kevin parked where the FedEx truck had been, under the magnolias. Our two-year-old jumped from the pool and flung himself at Daddy, soaking Kevin's front with his slippery seal body. After they played for a while, and Cal's attention drifted back to his floating toys, Kevin caught sight of the paperback on the porch. He picked it up.

"Read it if you want," I said. "I'm going to pass."

He went inside and stayed long enough for the magnolias' umbrella-shaped shadows to tilt across the yard and cover the pool. I wrapped a towel around my shivering son, thinking about the manila envelope my father had given me in Chicago—his "chapter" about my mother. That was eight years ago. I'd shipped his pages home with my research and thrown them out unread when I finally unpacked. His pearls on Mel would be somewhere in the paperback he'd paid a vanity publisher to print.

Kevin returned, red-faced with anger, as I was dumping pool water in the alley beside our house. His hands were empty. He lifted Cal from the porch and hugged him.

"I'm throwing it out," he said.

I dropped the plastic pool onto the grass. "Don't."

"He's like some blubbering Nazi—*I didn't know what was going on! I didn't mean to hurt anyone!*"

"Put it in a box," I said.

"It's obscene."

"Put the box in the basement."

"You shouldn't read it."

"Maybe I'll read it when he's dead."

A year later I was pregnant again—and thrilled. We had wanted another child, had been *trying,* as the saying goes. For months I'd used the calendar in our checkbook as a fertility chart, circling the first day of my periods, marking days we had sex with an *x.*

"I think you should put stars on the sex days," Kevin said.

"It's not a rating system, sweetie," I said. "I just want to see what's happening with my eggs and your sperm."

"Ooo, I love when you talk biology."

Now we were back at the gynecologist's together. I lay on an exam table, an ultrasound technician smearing clear jelly on my quarter-moon stomach. Kevin pulled a chair close and stroked my arm as the tech produced a gadget that looked like a vacuum attachment—a transducer, in the lingo we'd mastered our first time through, at sneak previews of our now three-year-old son—and began pressing and probing my greased middle. The transducer generated and received sound waves that translated into computer images. We three watched galaxies come in and out of focus on the monitor at the tech's side.

"There's the heartbeat," she said, momentarily halting her search. Kevin leaned down and kissed me, eyes brimming. I knew from my checkbook chart that I was fourteen weeks along—past the pistachio and tadpole stages, with a recognizably human-looking creature floating in my uterus. And there was the little muscle pumping blood inside its translucent form.

The tech continued her duties with the transducer, making notes. After a while she stopped the probe again.

"There you go," she said.

Kevin and I stared at the screen. The fetus had flipped around, maybe in response to the pressure on my abdomen, and now faced us.

"Do you see?" the tech asked.

"See what?" Kevin said, an edge of concern in his voice.

"Or don't you want to know the gender?"

She'd already pointed out various fetal organs, and though Kevin and I had made happy little comments about each constellation, a pea-size pancreas and lima-bean lungs looked about the same to us.

"We want to know," I said.

The tech smiled. "It's a girl."

And then Kevin and I were laughing, crying, reaching for each other—as oblivious to our surroundings as lovers in a first embrace. I'd been saying for months that it would be fine to have another boy, it would be great, imagine brothers romping on the beach together, picture them snuggled under covers in the boy-style bedroom in our bungalow. I'd recited my mantra to friends and neighbors, and Kevin and I left it at that. He knew I couldn't put words to the other possibility.

It's a girl.

One night, as I neared my due date, I woke from restless sleep with a dream image carried over to consciousness: A full-term fetus folded inside a pillowy womb, its blue umbilical roped around its neck. In the morning Kevin drove me to the doctor. I told her what I'd dreamed, and after she'd checked me outside and in, reporting that my growing girl was in perfect shape and position for delivery any day, she sent me—for my peace of mind—to the hospital next door to get an ultra-high-tech ultrasound scan.

Onto a huge screen in the hospital's exam room the attendant projected lifesize pictures. "See?" she said, touching the monitor. "Your daughter's fine."

And she was, an eight-pounder like her brother, arriving in the last dusky hour of light in August 1997.

After I'd held her in those first astonishing moments of life, when every fact you might know about the sublime science of reproduction is overwhelmed by joy, relief, gratitude—by the transcendence of this commonplace miracle—a nurse carried my girl to a warming table steps from where I lay for the requisite toe count, wipe down and swaddling under lamps toasting the air to body temperature.

The doctor who'd delivered her was my gynecologist's partner, and we chatted as she worked between my legs. I could see the top of her head above a sheet draped across my knees, and beyond her I saw Kevin, tear-stained and euphoric, beside the nurses at the warming table.

"Everything okay down there?" I asked the doctor, anxious for her to finish so I could hold my baby again.

"Everything's fine," she said. "I had to make a small cut. I'm just sewing you up."

That was news. Delivering Cal four years earlier, my doctor had told me that she and her partners didn't routinely give episiotomies—the cuts doctors make to ease the passage of a baby's head and shoulders. A small vaginal rip heals more quickly than a slice and stitches, she'd explained. She would let nature take its course, as long as the birth proceeded normally.

Which it had with Cal—I hadn't been cut. So why, I now asked, was I given an episiotomy for this much less arduous birth?

"The cord was around the baby's neck," the doctor said, raising her head to face me over the sheet. "I had to get her out as quickly as possible."

At his post across the room, Kevin had heard. Our eyes met, and I answered his shocked expression with a laugh. We'd been together for almost sixteen years, a span that stretched from our early twenties to our late thirties, from carefree self-involvement to hands-on parenthood. We knew each other as no one else could know either of us. Every shared experience echoed through all that had come before.

I was wheeled to a room in the maternity ward with my new bundle in my arms, and Kevin went home to spend the night with Cal. When they arrived the next morning I was sitting up in bed, my dozing daughter cradled against me. At Hoag Hospital in Newport Beach, where both of my children were born, a maternity patient could choose to keep her baby in her room for the very short hospital stay allowed by insurance companies—I was checked in and wheeled out in less than twenty-four hours both times—or send her neonate down the hall to the nursery, to sleep and cry out and be soothed by staff attending rows of identical bassinets. Touring Hoag's maternity ward while I was pregnant with Cal, Kevin and I had stared at rows of sleeping Buddha babies in the nursery and mumbled something between ourselves. "Oh, you say that *now*," the eavesdropping tour guide interjected, "but you'll see. You're going to want your sleep, Mom—and that means putting your baby *in there!*" A nugget of parental wisdom, like many before and more to come, that we rejected as fool's gold.

Cal, now four years old, climbed onto my hospital bed and stared at the little red face pressed to my chest.

"What's her name?" he asked. For months he'd known I was carrying a girl—we'd talked about his sister constantly from the time her gender and general health were confirmed by amniocentesis. But Kevin and I had kept her name to ourselves, just as we'd done when I was carrying Cal. I wanted my new baby to be the first to hear it.

"Lily," I said, reaching out to draw Cal closer.

He gently touched the black hair plastered to her scalp, then leaned over and whispered, "I love you, Lily."

* * *

I had learned the details of my own birth from foggy photocopies given to me with my father's permission by the records department of Chicago's Michael Reese Hospital. In the medical style of the day—at least for an urban American middle-class white woman—my mother had been given local and general anesthesia at the start of what was characterized, on a hospital worksheet, as a "long, hard labor." She'd been knocked out cold to give birth, then pumped with more medicine to stimulate contractions in her drugged slumber. After chemically managing her eighteen-hour labor and performing an episiotomy, my mother's doctor made a "low forceps del. of living female." From a pediatrician's report dated four days later, I learned that I had "a complete fracture through the middle third of the clavicle with slight overriding of the bony parts"—the slash-and-grab delivery had broken my collarbone.

I thought about my mother as I shuffled from bed to bathroom to glider those first days home with Lily, middle name Lady. Mildred maiden name Lady would have had to buck the zeitgeist in 1958 to give birth to me in any manner other than she did, or to have used her breasts postpartum for the function that determined their form. Each day of her weeklong maternity stay at Michael Reese she was given masses of aspirin and a daily blast of Seconal, probably to dull the pain of engorged breasts unsuckled, and instructed "to lie on abdomen at least four hours daily," probably to help deflate an empty uterus that would have been stimulated to contract by a nursing baby—part of a hormonal checks-and-balances system as old as the species. The last note about me on record, other than the pediatrician's description of my broken collarbone, was made shortly after my arrival: "Baby to nursery in arms of nurse."

Poor Mel.

She'd had the misfortune—the cosmic bad timing—to bring her children into the world in the blink of American medical history when obstetrical practices contravened evolution and common sense. What women had managed among themselves for tens of thousands of years was briefly transformed into a male-orchestrated *operation* akin to a butcher's procedures with fresh kill.

By the time I waddled into the maternity ward in the nineties, the pendulum had swung back toward ancient wisdom. Doctors recommended prepping for delivery with breathing and relaxation techniques, and tutored first-timers in the health benefits of breast feeding for both baby and mom. We urban American middle-class white women had choices our mothers couldn't have imagined. Underwater birth, anyone? Soft music and low lights? If you shopped docs and hospitals you could customize, at least in the planning stages, or opt out of the system completely and hire a midwife to run the show at home.

Long before my first mysterious due date approached, I knew I wasn't a candidate for "natural" birth—I wanted a baby, not an endurance test. And once my labor progressed past the gas-pains stage, once I was flopping around on a hospital bed like the catch of the day, cursing with each contraction's atomic bloom, tense with anticipation in the ever-shrinking pauses between lengthening spasms, I happily accepted anesthesia delivered straight to my spine (an "epidural," in the lingo). The wonder drugs almost instantly cut away nine-tenths of labor's agony, leaving me with enough muscle control to push when the time came, and the presence of mind to enjoy it.

My doctor, significantly to me, was a woman—near my age and a mother herself. She hugged my tearful husband when Cal had taken his first breaths, and kissed me as she laid my baby on top of me for the skin-to-skin reassurance of each other's existence that surely echoed through our chromosomes.

Lucky me.

And luckily for Cal a nursing aide was sent to my room. Her brusque bony hands showed me what to do with my newly heavy breasts and that hungry little mouth. I was full of fantasies and devoid of skill—as awkward in my way as an adolescent boy making his first fumbling efforts with real live mammaries. I'd tried to learn breast-feeding from books but what I needed was this, a woman twice my age, a mother herself, showing me how to position myself and my baby, telling me not to worry, I was doing great, everyone goes through this, the pain is normal and it will pass, you have to be patient, you have to be strong, just stick with it and you'll see, *what's hurting you now will be your greatest joy*—

I thought about my mother.

I thought about my mother.

I brought my daughter home in the month of August, as Mel had thirty-eight years before. She'd traveled from Chicago to Kingsport when I was a recognizably human-looking creature folded inside her pillowy womb, to be with her father during his last days and attend his funeral at the First Baptist Church on Church Circle. Back in her townhouse on Elm Street, feeding and caring for a newborn while attending the needs and demands of her firstborn, she would have had her mother with her, helping her.

I had Kevin to help with my newborn and firstborn, and never wanted anyone else. I'd turned thirty-nine a few days after Lily was born, and I had felt, looking around my flower- and friend-filled home, my daughter in my arms and son hovering nearby, like a long-distance runner breaking the tape at the end of a race. Here was the love and intimacy I had craved for as long as I could remember, the mountain-high, river-wide stuff of pop songs, come to me in my fourth decade—in motherhood. I knew that whatever happened to me from now on happened to *us*. We were mother and father, sister and brother: My family.

By the end of 1997 we'd sold our house and moved across the country. Kevin had gone to New York to hunt freelance work and returned with a job offer—the *Sports Illustrated* editor who'd given him assignments for years, including a story about girls' basketball that took him to Iowa as I left for Kingsport in 'eighty-eight—had a colleague who needed staff. As parents of two children under age five, our priorities restacked along their budding timelines, we said yes to medical benefits, a 401(k), paychecks rolling in like tides. We'd had a twelve-year run at the beach. Now we traded freelance freedom for button-down stability, waving goodbye to our spreading magnolias, to the Australian willow and silvery eucalyptus that had climbed far above the upside-down V roof on a house that looked like the ones little kids draw.

Our first year in the city was tough. Kevin was absent many nights, working the long hours required at a weekly magazine, as I nursed baby Lily and comforted disoriented preschooler Cal, shuffling from bed to couch to darkened windows in a drafty loft. We arrived in January, not the ideal month for a splashdown with tots. Days, I pushed a stroller around lower Manhattan, making the circuit familiar to all full-time child-tenders: from school to park to grocery store to laundry room, round and round she goes, when she stops, give her Merlot . . . The blank pages at the back of my Week-At-a-Glance, where a decade earlier I'd tallied my earnings, filled with addresses and phone numbers of pediatricians, twenty-four-hour pharmacies, neighbors with kids, babysitters recommended by moms, children's sports and arts activities.

When we'd made our way through a set of seasons, the tree limbs below our windows bearing green-tipped promises of another hard-earned spring, I found myself—as I ran endless errands, as I lay abed half listening for Kevin's key in the door lock—thinking about my father. My mother was with me daily now, her self-portraits by my desk, her grandparents sternly overseeing a bookshelf, her juvenilia hanging in the kids' room (Indian Brave, Tom Sawyer, Birddog and Kitten had gotten museum-quality restorations, too). She was a fixture in my home and, inevitably, a specter in my conversations with other moms.

My dead mother was part of my life, but my living father had receded to the vanishing point. From the few friends my brother and I still shared I knew how my story played in Chicago: I was the black sheep. All that braying I'd done about my mom when I was twenty-nine, all those questions I'd asked, the dig, dig, digging with my cloven hooves—proof of my selfishness, my cruelty to my father. Same rap his sister Lois had phoned in from Palm Beach when I was pregnant with Cal. I was a lousy daughter, he was a wronged dad. Case closed.

I thought about him as I strolled through my days, as I lay awake when I should have slept. I replayed scenes from Evanston, and from the years my low-rent young adulthood ran parallel to his high-rise bankruptcy, and from our bitter review of my mother's life and death. I thought about him without much emotion—in pictures, mostly, and then in the bigger picture of my own family, my happiness and responsibilities as a mother of two. And I decided to find out if there might be a peaceful way to put my kids and my father in a room together. Never mind what had happened or what might come. If children teach you anything, it's how to live in the present tense. I was learning and relearning that lesson every day. Maybe I could use it to salve an old wound. How hard could it be for us to spend a few hours in each other's company?

I called him. His girlfriend answered. After we made cautious small talk she told me that my father was sleeping, and suggested I call back another time. I went ahead and told her what I was thinking—that maybe Kevin and I would bring the kids to Chicago for a few days, and maybe all of us could have a meal together, or walk by the lake, or sit on a park bench. Whatever was comfortable for him, I said.

She said she didn't think this was a good time for a visit. She said I should wait until my father was "feeling better." My father was eighty-six years old. His girlfriend was fifty-six. I was forty—older than she'd been when she accepted her widowed boyfriend's gift of his dead wife's wedding ring.

I didn't call back. Instead, I booked four round-trip tickets and reserved a hotel room near their apartment. We left New York on July 2, 1999—Cal's sixth birthday, the trip a surprise revealed at breakfast with a candle-topped cake. Lily was almost two, still in diapers but a walking, talking part of the group. I didn't tell the kids about meeting their grandfather, not wanting to spark expectations of any kind. We were taking our maiden voyage together to the city where Mommy was born. We'd see the sights, have some fun: Case opened.

It calmed me to have my children with me, to have Kevin at my side, as we made our way around my hometown like tourists—visiting Lincoln Park and Navy Pier, the Art Institute and the Field Museum, Oak Street Beach, the Hancock Building, the Sears Tower. We window-shopped the stretch of Michigan Avenue that civic boosters call the Magnificent Mile, and I marveled, like any newcomer, at the flowering median islands and other cosmetic touch-ups fashioned by da son of da mayor of my youth, King Richard the First. As luck would have it, it was the summer of "Cows on Parade"—the sidewalks sporting life-size fiberglass bovines, each fanciful artwork a perfect photo op for a tourist family with a kindergartener and an almost-two.

Kevin and I stood at the windows of our hotel room with our children in our arms as Fourth of July fireworks exploded over the lake, streaking the glass skin of the high-rises nearby. The next morning, with two empty days between us and our flight home, I called my father. His girlfriend answered.

"Hi Judy," I said, trying to hit cheerful notes. "I'm here with Kevin and the kids. I was hoping we could all get together."

She put me on hold. I thought she was summoning my father, or carrying the phone to him, but it was her voice that returned, blurting without preamble, "Pamela, your father passed away last night."

Died, I would later learn, as fireworks exploded outside his aerie.

Was, in fact, still lying in her bed when I called: Judy was waiting for the funeral parlor's legmen to come take him away. She'd tended him during the night with morphine from an eye-dropper, comforting him as he woozily echoed the explosions, *"boom . . . boom . . . boom."* I would later learn.

Right then I put the phone down. And when I was ready to speak to her again, ten minutes later, Judy was screening her calls.

She would screen me out that day and evening, and through-out the following day and evening, as Kevin and I dialed and re-dialed, leaving message after message asking for nothing more than the bare facts of what came next. The Christian Science Church doesn't marry or bury—the body's desires and destiny not their thing. So we called my father's home and kept calling, try-ing to find out if there would be a service for him, and where, and when. His girlfriend didn't answer or call us back.

My father died on a Saturday night. We were booked to fly home Monday. On Sunday, Kevin called his boss at *Sports Illustrated* to explain that Chicago had become Limbo, and he didn't know when he'd get out. Monday before dawn I slipped from our hotel room to buy the papers and check the obits. Nothing. But on Tuesday I found my father's name in the columns of death notices in the *Chicago Tribune* and the *Sun-Times*. Unlike obituaries, which are written by reporters, death notices are submitted by survivors and cost a few coins per word. The notice for **Marin, Allan Marshall,** was identical in both papers.

Top billing went to Judy, to whom he was attached as "devoted partner." He was described as a "loving father" and a "grandfather of two"—that last a reference to my kids, and a news nugget of sorts to me. At least now I knew for sure that my father and his girlfriend had received their birth announcements. They'd answered the engraved card-plus-photo we'd sent at Lily's debut, like the one we sent out celebrating Cal, with stone silence.

No mention of my mother in the little prose poem constructed by my loving father's devoted partner.

I drank coffee in the hotel restaurant and used my paper placemat to write a eulogy for the funeral, set for Thursday, listed in Marin, Allan Marshall's death notice. Then I went upstairs to my sleeping family.

The funeral parlor my father was taken to from his girlfriend's bed was in the ritzy Gold Coast neighborhood off the northern tip of Michigan Avenue. Two blocks away, on Elm Street, was the townhouse he and my mother had invested with sweat equity, to which they'd brought their son and then their daughter fresh from Michael Reese Hospital's maternity ward. Elm Street had been Nellie Lady's home, too, her splashdown up North. It wasn't hard to imagine them—my still-youngish mother and middle-aged father and newly widowed grandmother—pushing a stroller along the neighborhood's leafy streets on a bright summer day like the one that brought me there.

We arrived for the service early, wearing dark clothes and dress shoes bought that morning at Marshall Field's in Water Tower Plaza. I went straight to Judy and embraced her. Without a hint of surprise or embarrassment at seeing me, she described my father's last hours, his quiet death as fireworks *boomed*.

My brother was there, but we kept our distance, though some of his friends and their parents came to me to say the kinds of things that get said at funerals.

Helen Rosenberg, whom I'd known since I was Cal's age, had come with her father, Max. Her mother had slipped far enough down Alzheimer's slope to have been left with a minder in the house on Judson Avenue that the Rosenbergs had loaned me for a few weeks in 'eighty-eight.

And there were my cousins from the southside—my father's brother's kids—who'd shared our tawny Thanksgiving turkeys and clove-speckled Easter hams in the big white house in Evanston. My Uncle Leonard had been senior associate at Allan Marin & Associates—the one who'd thrown away my mom's picture files so long ago.

Here was Tom, Leonard's eldest; and second son Peter; and Diedre, who was my age. All three were married, with children ranging from Diedre's six-month-old to Peter's college baseball player. All three had stuck close to their roots in the suburban fringe the papers called "Chicagoland," getting together with their widowed mom on holidays. It had been decades since I'd seen them, but now here was Diedre sharing a jar of her baby's apricots with Lily, here was Peter's collegian squatting next to Cal for a game of tic-tac-toe.

When it was time to sit and listen, I settled on a small couch off to the side of the rows of chairs facing the podium. Cal fitted himself against me, and Kevin held Lily on his lap. I could stretch out my arm and touch all three of them—my little group gathered on an upholstered lifeboat, watching the funeral barge roll past.

There were two eulogists, a businessman and a lawyer. I dimly remembered their names and faces from our years on Forest Avenue. The businessman told stories of his long friendship with my father, recalling with particular warmth my father's "childlike exuberance." The lawyer spoke in a similar vein. Both paid homage to Judy and to my brother, who was given a large American flag folded into a triangle, a military honor.

Not a word about my mother.

Nor so much as a glance at me from the podium, though I'd caught both speakers glowering my way before the service began.

So be it. I touched the paper placemat tucked in my new black shoe and decided to leave it there. My father had made choices, as we all do, and been storm-tossed by fortune. By then I knew that his beloved father Jacob, hero of oft-told tales, had come to the New World from Poland, not Alsace-Lorraine, and that Jacob-the-tailor was Jewish, as was his wife Gertrude. When Gertrude was mad at her husband, according to an in-law, she'd hiss, *"Jacob! Don't be such a Jew!"*

Marin, my common-in-Spanish name—*mah-reen* to the cooks and busboys I'd worked with—would have been Marynowicz, or maybe Marynowski. Would have been trimmed and Anglicized at Ellis Island.

My father's sister Lois, of the phone tirade from Palm Beach, and her retired-doctor husband, her grown children, her grand-children—all Jewish. Why weren't we?

Because Gertrude Marin converted to Christian Science, and took her elder son along for the ride. Not her husband—*Jew!*—or Lois and Leonard, her other kids. Just Allan, her firstborn.

My father had loved his father—anyone who heard him talk about Jacob knew that—but he went to church with his mother, to hear the gospel according to Mary Baker Eddy. And there he learned that illness and death were products of "mortal mind."

Illness and death were bad thinking, basically. To be un-thunk.

He must have been scared, trying to think away my mother's cancer. He must have been scared as he went about his business—off to work, off to church—while she suffered for months in California, and met death alone in a hospital bed.

Fear and guilt—the coward's bedfellows: He must have carried them to the end of his days.

That's why he purged our home and family life of her as soon as she was gone.

That's why he shut me out at twenty-nine rather than let my mother back in with me.

Fear and guilt kept him estranged from one of his two children, unknown to his only grandkids, unto his last heartbeat.

He made choices. We all do. And when it came to his own illness, as his own death approached, he chose the miracles of modern medicine for himself—surgeries, checkups, anesthetics, prescription pain relief. Non-denominational science.

And of course he had a devoted partner at his side, as my mother did not.

We went home to New York. I let a month pass, then I called Judy. I waited until my kids were asleep, until I'd had a glass of red to calm me and reviewed with Kevin what I planned to say. Then I dialed the number in Chicago I'd been calling since my teens.

"Hi Judy."

"Well hello there," she said, and we began a cautious give-and-take, a kind of gentle interview, really, with me lobbing mild queries and Judy recounting a trip she'd taken after the funeral, to stay with friends, and her decision to go back to work recently, how that had helped her feel better. She said she was concerned about my brother, she hoped he'd be all right—he was still so deeply, so painfully, in mourning. I let that pass.

After fifteen minutes or so I asked if my father had a will.

The interview halted for a moment. Then, "Yes."

"Who's the executor?"

"I am."

"Can I get a copy of it?"

"I don't have his will, Pamela," she said sharply, and for the first time in years I craved a cigarette. I'd quit smoking on my thirty-third birthday, when Kevin and I decided to start a family. That same year, and for the same reason, we'd gone to a courthouse in California and come home married.

I drew a deep breath and began the little speech I'd prepared. I wasn't looking for money, I said, if my father had any. Or any of his personal effects, his possessions. But there were some things in her apartment that had belonged to my mother and her mother—my Grandmother *Lady*. The maternal line. These things had a powerful hold on my imagination, I said. I wanted them for myself, yes, I'd be lying if I pretended otherwise, but what I wanted most was to be able to give them to my children.

I mentioned the lace tablecloth my grandmother crocheted.

The phone was silent.

I mentioned a few pieces of jewelry I knew my mother had particularly treasured.

"Now *Pamela*," Judy said, "*I* don't know which pieces of jewelry were your mother's!"

I could have asked if she really thought I was trying to rip her off—to steal her jewels by claiming them as my mom's.

I could have said that I had photographs of Mrs. Allan Marin in her Sunday best, posed in front of our house in Evanston, wearing necklaces and brooches her husband gave her during their twenty-two-year marriage.

But I had my answer, and it tightened my throat. This was too ugly, too ridiculous. I said goodbye and wept as I hadn't in years—silently at first, then racked with sobs, each gulped breath a bellows blast on kindling. Sounding like some furry animal with its leg in a trap.

Two days later a copy of my father's will arrived in the mail. The lawyer who'd prepared it informed me in a cover letter that he "would be glad to answer any questions you may have but please do not contact Judy . . . with respect to your father's estate."

I called his office in Chicago. "I have a question for you, Mr. Silbert," I said. "Whose lawyer are you?"

"I don't know what you mean," he replied.

"You wrote my father's will. And now you've sent me a letter as his girlfriend's representative."

"I'm the lawyer for the estate."

"Now I don't know what *you* mean," I said.

"Well, I'm kind of wearing two hats here," he said, and then he said a bunch of stuff I didn't bother to take notes on—lawyerly dissembling.

"This is silly," I said when I'd heard enough. "My father didn't have any money. We're not talking about money."

"Well, as you can see in Section Two—"

"I'm calling you for two reasons," I said. "Their names are Cal and Lily. They're my kids. I don't know if you have kids, Mr. Silbert, but even if you don't, you probably have things in your house that were handed down to you from your parents—things that were maybe handed down from *their* parents, or maybe date back even further. These things may have monetary value, or they may not, but that's not the point. That's not what gives them value *to you*. You value them because they're *part of your family's story*. They come to you from your ancestors, and you'll pass them to the next generation. It's the handing down that makes them sacred. Do you have any things like that?"

I heard papers shuffle. I heard the lawyer sigh. "Judy was very disturbed by your call," he said.

"So was I."

"She's grieving for your father," he said, "and she knows you are not."

"And how would she know that, sir?"

M y southside cousins got in touch.

Diedre sent notes and photos of her long-awaited baby boy. Peter shipped boxes of presents for Cal and Lily, with pictures of his college ballplayer son tucked inside. Tom, a father of three, who like our fathers was an adman in the Loop, became an e-mail buddy.

"Dear Pamela or should I say Pam?" he wrote, opening our exchange. That made me smile. My cousins were strangers to me, yet the blood tie drew us to one another. I was surprised how much I looked forward to hearing from them, how often my kids mentioned theirs.

A year after my father's funeral I took my family back to the Midwest to hang with the cousins, who'd organized a weekend of backyard baseball and barbecues. We arrived to find carnival workers setting up shop in the parking lot of the hotel I'd booked, a coincidence that delighted my seven-year-old and almost-three. That night I stood with my cousin Tom, whose coloring and features were similar to mine, whose backstory ran parallel to mine from page one, as my son and his son, my daughter and his daughter, screamed together in the flickering lights of thrill rides. And I thought: I want this. I want Cal and Lily to have branching roots surrounding the taproot. I want a sturdier family tree for myself, yes, but most of all I want it for my children.

We came home from that trip with a photo album my cousins had made for me by culling their own picture stocks. The opening pages held black-and-whites from the fifties—shots of my mother, mostly, posed with her parents by the townhouse on Elm Street, and with her new husband in stylish Mag Mile duds. Then it was on to the sixties, when my cousins and my brother and I were snapped as we played on suburban lawns, and as we sat at the kids' table for holiday meals in the big white house in Evanston.

A few months after we got home, a box arrived for me. I carried it up four flights to my drafty loft and unpacked bubblewrapped photos in expensive frames, carefully preserved diplomas and certificates, news clips in plastic sheet protectors. Mementoes of my father's life. He'd left them at the local printer he paid to publish his *pensées*. A file-cleaning clerk had called the only Marin in advertising in Chicago she could find—Tom Marin. A note from Tom explained the contents' provenance.

I put the box in a closet and called my cousin.

"I've had that stuff for a while," he said. "I wasn't sure what to do with it."

"Did he send you the thing he wrote?" I asked.

"Yeah, he did."

"Did you read it?"

"Nah."

"Me either," I said, and we moved on—to our kids, family gossip, the headlines. Before we hung up I asked Tom if people ever thought he was Jewish. I said I got asked all the time. Often it was just assumed, as when a mom at Cal's school recently mentioned that I might try basting the Passover brisket in kosher wine this year—she'd tried it, and it turned out great!

Tom laughed. He'd wanted to have that conversation with his father, he said, and tried many times. "All Leonard would say was, 'Tom, look in the mirror.'"

We went back to Chicago the next summer and stayed at Tom's house, and again the following year. Cal slept in his cousin John's room, Lily bunked with Tom's younger daughter, Ariel. During that third get-together, in August 2002, my cousins and their spouses and kids and widowed mom sang a rousing "Happy Birthday" to Lily, who sat blushing over a platter of cupcakes decorated with Disney princesses. She had just turned five. Cal was nine. By then my kids knew the sights in my hometown almost as well as their southside cousins did.

On the last day of vacation I rode a commuter train to the Loop with Tom, kissed him as he headed off to work, then took the el to Howard Street, where I transferred to a Skokie Swift. Then I got scared and called Kevin, who was back at Tom's house organizing the kids for an outing.

"I don't know if I can do this," I said.

"You don't have to."

"I want to."

The line was quiet for a while. We didn't need to fill it.

"Okay," I said, finally. "I'll be back by dinner."

"We'll be here," Kevin said.

I dropped my cell phone into my shoulder bag and got in the first cab in line at the Skokie train station. The driver looked like Nick Nolte after a bender. When I told him where I wanted to go he grunted, lowered the sunglasses nesting in his matted bangs and got us onto Gross Point Road. Heading north, we crossed Golf Road near the corner where I'd crashed my dad's gray Benz one rainy night. To the left on Golf, no more than a mile away, was Harms Woods Forest Preserve, where I'd sat at a picnic table with my tape recorder and notepad in 'eighty-eight. That was fourteen years ago. My father had fired a warning shot that day. *"Why are you doing this to me?"* he'd yelled, slamming his hands on the tabletop. Soon after, I'd discovered why my questions rattled him. In time I would understand how he came to fancy himself the true subject of my inquiries.

A short jog from that picnic spot, on the corner of Golf and Harms Road, was where Peebles' Stables had been—my destination nearly every day from the time I was fourteen, when my parents bought Helluva Note for me, until I left high school without benefit of a diploma in the middle of senior year. From fourteen to seventeen—the first years after my mom died—I'd come to this western district of Chicagoland to ride my horse. Ferried by my father, or by drivers who picked me up hitching. Sometimes I took the bus to Old Orchard Shopping Center and walked the last mile west on Golf. Sometimes I rode my Raleigh all the way out from Evanston. I came here nearly every day of the first three years after my mom died, a thousand days, give or take, but I never came *here*—

"This is good," I said as Nick Nolte turned off Gross Point Road.

"Here?" He braked at the foot of a long driveway shaded by old trees. I was out of the cab before he stopped the meter, handing bills through his open window, digging in my bag for shades and a hat, stepping quickly through patches of sun and shadow on the springy sod beside the pavement.

The driveway led to a small brick building. I went in and handed the clerk a note I'd prepared so I wouldn't have to find out what would happen if I tried to talk. She took the note to her files and returned with two maps—one of the whole cemetery, with its square and rhomboid sections like blank puzzle pieces fitted around inky lagoons, the other a cross-hatched, densely numbered map of the Ivy Section, where my mother was buried in 1973, the only other time I was here. Thirty years ago. The clerk used a yellow highlighter to mark my mother's plot, and the route I should take to get to her.

Down the highlighted access road, looking across undulant lawns bright with noon light, looking at old trees clumped like mourners, looking at flowerbeds and poodle-cut shrubs, little flags and lawn ornaments and bouquets in all stages of decay.

The highlighted plot was in a corner of its puzzle piece. As I stepped to the stone lying flat in the grass I saw with a jolt that below my block-lettered surname were the names of both of my parents. So my father had bought a single marker in 'seventy-three, planning to be interred with his wife when the time came. But of course he hadn't been. My mother's side of the stone was cut with the dates of her birth and death; his side listed birth date only. I hadn't thought to ask his girlfriend about the dispensation of his remains when I saw her at the memorial service I'd learned about from death notices in the *Trib* and *Sun-Times*. It didn't matter to me. She could have them.

I sat in the grass for a long, long time, summoning wisps of memories of my mother's funeral, at the First Baptist Church of Evanston, and the drive we'd taken, following a hearse, in the big brown Benz that was my father's last luxury car, and the final ceremony here, under a white canopy, that sent her casket underground. What little I remembered from that time-buried Ides of March had come back to me the year I studied her life. At twenty-nine. Now I was forty-four. In six years I would be as old as she ever was.

Of course I wept. And when I was done I fished a notebook from my bag and wrote *Dear Mel*. Listening to insect buzz and mower rumble. Watching bees embroider the air.

I'm here, I wrote, where your story ended. I know you hoped for something after this—another kind of existence, in another realm. With God. I've always had trouble with that word. God and its corollaries: faith, prayer, salvation. When you were dying those words took you away from us. When you were dying those words carried you away from your home, away from your husband and children, away from your mother. You were seeking God's salvation. You believed in the magical power of prayer. I have tried to understand your flight of faith.

I'm still trying.

Mary Baker Eddy had one child, with the first of her three husbands. A boy. When he was six years old his mother gave him to the servant who had tended him from birth, and a few years later her former servant and nominal son moved to Minnesota. Bye! Mary Baker not-yet-Eddy lived in New Hampshire then. She didn't see her boy again until she was older than you ever got to be, and he was almost as old as I am now.

Mother Eddy. Queen of her Mother Church.

I went back to Kingsport recently, a social call, to see Dorothy and the others, to walk around your hometown and think about you. Dorothy's past 80 now, sharp as ever, brave in her pain. One night as we sat in her den, beside the smoky photo of her mother, our backs to the darkened park where you two played with dolls, she said, "I never will forget when we went to that funeral parlor."

We'd been talking about you. I said, "In Chicago?"

" 'Course I know it's the big city, and they do things different."

"Yes."

"Down here, you know, we have one way of doin' things . . ." Her voice trailed off. I waited.

Dorothy said, "You don't remember goin' there, do you?"

"Not at all. Total blank."

And I could see that she didn't want to go on, didn't want to put words to the pictures in her mind, but she had to now—for me.

"Well," she said, "we went in and said, 'We're here to see Mildred.' And the man led us down this long dark hallway, flippin' on the lights as he went. And he got to this one room and he stopped and read the name on the card by the door, and that was it. He opened the door and flipped on the light."

Her voice wavered. I watched her blind fingers stumble around her lap.

"She was lyin' there . . ." Her voice gave out again.

"In the dark," I prompted.

"In the dark."

"Alone."

"All alone."

"And I was there," I said.

"Oh, Pamela. You just went crazy."

"How so?"

"You were hysterical," Dorothy said, "seein' your momma like that. You just broke to pieces."

The next day I went up to Oak Hill Cemetery with your cousin Helen

Stone. Helen's a table-tennis champ these days, traveling the senior circuit, bringing home trophies and anecdotes, looking decades younger than her age. We talked about you, of course, and about her mother Grace— Nellie's sister. Helen said, "You have to get a little older to appreciate your momma," and I knew exactly what she meant.

I climbed to the monument inscribed L A D Y and sat on it for a while, relishing the verdant view of misty hills at dusk, the oniony smell of the grass. That spot was the last stop on my whirlwind tour of your life, Act One. It was where I learned that Nellie had a second child, a sister for you, who only lived six days.

I knelt and kissed the cold stone inscribed with your mother's name and dates, then moved to the marker where your father's casket was lowered as you watched with me, suspended in your womb, six weeks shy of a difficult delivery.

I kissed Virginia Ruth's stone and then I noticed a dent in the grass farther down the line, and shuffled to it on my knees:

A stone no bigger than a book, sunken by time and the elements, inscribed, simply, L.

A place holder. On a fourth plot. How about that.

I didn't say anything about it to Helen, or to Dorothy when we got back. I haven't even mentioned it to Kevin yet. I wanted to tell you first. That's why I came here, after thirty years. To tell you you're going home.

You belong in Kingsport, in that rusty Tennessee clay dirt, beside your smooth-talking father and long-suffering mother and the baby sister whose firefly life flamed in a mock Tudor on Compton Terrace. Near the Baptists of Church Circle. Near the friends and relatives who gave me their memories of you along with every scrap of yours they could find so I'd have something to hold on to, since I didn't have you.

There's no reason on earth for you to be stuck in the ground out here alone. Your story should end among your people, as your life did not. I'm taking you home. You watch.

Thank you

Nina Collins for your support and advocacy; Martha Levin
for the green light; and Elizabeth Stein, my editorial soul sister.
Not a bad penny, Liz—a rabbit's foot.

About the Author

Pamela Marin has written for *Playboy, Redbook, Parents, Parenting, Ladies' Home Journal* and the *Los Angeles Times*. A former staff writer for *The Orange County Register,* she has been featured on *The Oprah Winfrey Show.* She lives in New York with her husband and children.

She can be reached at www.motherlandmemoir.com.